Islamic Surveys 19

Muslim Neoplatonists

An Introduction to the Thought of the Brethren of Purity
(*Ikhwān al-Ṣafāʾ*)

IAN RICHARD NETTON

EDINBURGH UNIVERSITY PRESS

First published 1982 in hardback by
George Allen & Unwin (Publishers) Ltd

Reprinted in paperback 1991 with corrections by
Edinburgh University Press, 22 George Square, Edinburgh

Typeset in 11 on 12 point Ehrhardt,
and printed in Great Britain by
Page Bros Ltd, Norwich

British Library Cataloguing in Publication Data
Netton, Ian Richard
Muslim Neoplatonists.
1. Ikhwān al-Ṣafā' 2. Philosophy, Islamic
I. Title
181'.9 BY746

ISBN 0 7486 0251 8

To my wife Sue, my mother
Olive and the memory of my father Frederick
with love and gratitude

Preface and Acknowledgements

After a lull of some years, interest in *The Epistles of the Brethren of Purity* (*Rasā'il Ikhwān al-Ṣafā'*) has recently revived. This revival has been marked by the appearance of an increasing number of articles in various journals as well as by three major works on the Ikhwān by European authors in French, German and Italian: *La Philosophie des Iḫwān al-Ṣafā'* (1975) by Yves Marquet, *Arabische Philosophie und Wissenschaft in der Enzyklopädie Kitāb Iḫwān aṣ-ṣafā' (III): Die Lehre von Seele und Intellekt* (1975) by Susanne Diwald, and *L'Enciclopedia dei Fratelli della Purità* (1978) by Alessandro Bausani (see Bibliography for publication details). A significant point in this renaissance of Ikhwān studies was the symposium on the Ikhwān al-Ṣafā' held in Rome at the Palazzo Corsini on 25 and 26 October 1979 under the auspices of the Fondazione Leone Caetani of the Accademia Nazionale dei Lincei, at which I was privileged to read a paper beside the three scholars mentioned above.

It seems likely that the interest thus generated in the *Rasā'il* will continue and this book in English is an attempt to complement, in a small way, the three volumes to which I have already referred. To the best of my knowledge there exists no modern work in English devoted *entirely* to a study of the philosophy of the Ikhwān al-Ṣafā', though perhaps Seyyed Hossein Nasr has come closest to this with his book entitled *An Introduction to Islamic Cosmological Doctrines*, the first third of which deals with the Ikhwān (see Bibliography).

These Ikhwān al-Ṣafā' are as well known to an educated Arab as, say, the names of Descartes, Hegel and Wittgenstein are to the cultured European. This book is an introduction to their thought: it makes no claims to be comprehensive or to cover every facet of the Ikhwān's doctrine but seeks only to *introduce* the reader to some aspects of that doctrine. I hope that it will be useful not only to students of Arabic literature and Islamic philosophy but also to students of Western philosophy and theology who require some illustration of how the West has encountered the East on the stage of Neoplatonic thought. Unfortunately for the latter, there is still no translation into English of the entire *Rasā'il*, though a few individual epistles have been translated at various times.

The debts of gratitude which I have incurred in writing this book are many. First and foremost must be mentioned Professor M. A. Shaban, Head of the Department of Arabic and Islamic Studies at the University of Exeter. He has watched over and guided this work from its infancy, through a variety of stages, and without his inspiration, encouragement and scholarly advice it is unlikely that it would ever have been completed. I am grateful too, for help and advice from my departmental colleagues, Dr G. H. A. Juynboll and Mr J. R. Smart, Lecturers in Arabic and Islamic Studies at the University of Exeter; and from Professor the Revd Canon J. R. Porter, Professor of Theology in the University of Exeter, and Mr Cyril Cave, Senior Lecturer in Theology at the same university. Professor J. B. Segal, Professor of Semitic Languages in the University of London, generously helped me with some Syriac transliteration. I thank the editors of *Jerusalem Studies in Arabic and Islam*, Professors S. Pines and M. J. Kister, for permission to reprint, in a slightly emended and shortened form, as Chapter Six of this book, my article entitled 'Brotherhood versus Imāmate: Ikhwān al-Ṣafā' and the Ismā'īlīs', which appeared in volume 2 of their journal. I am also grateful to Thorsons Publishers Ltd of Wellingborough for permission to quote from *The Golden Verses of Pythagoras* translated by N. L. Redfield from the version of A. Fabre d'Olivet. My final thanks go to my editor, Mr John Hardy of George Allen & Unwin, for his unfailing care and efficiency in the production of this book.

IAN RICHARD NETTON
Lecturer in Arabic and Islamic Studies
University of Exeter
July 1980

Contents

We were sleepers in the cave of our father Adam.
(*Ikhwān al-Ṣafā'*)

CHAPTER ONE

The Ikhwān al-Ṣafā' and their Rasā'il

The group of medieval Arab philosophers known to Islamic history as the Brethren of Purity (*Ikhwān al-Ṣafā'*) has rightly been described as both an 'obscure puzzle' and a 'padlocked treasure'.[1] Their writings, presented in the form of epistles (*rasā'il*) are frequently complicated, repetitive and, at the same time, impressively encyclopedic. Their subject matter is vast and ranges from mathematics, music and logic, through mineralogy, botany and embryology, to philosophical and theological topics which are concluded by a treatise on magic. It is small wonder that many scholars, with only a few notable exceptions, have preferred to avoid textual exploration and exegesis; indeed, as one scholar points out, most previous research has been concerned instead with a positive identification of the authors of the *Rasā'il* and a definitive dating of their work.[2]

These interlocked themes of authorship and dating have been the source of frequent speculation over the years, and continue both to tantalise and to irritate: for *The Epistles of the Brethren of Purity* (*Rasā'il Ikhwān al-Ṣafā'*) remain one of the great works of Arabic literature about whose authors we know hardly anything. It is admitted that the epistles were written by a group of philosophers who called themselves Ikhwān al-Ṣafā', and traditionally agreed that this group lived in the Lower Mesopotamian river port of Baṣra during the tenth or eleventh century AD. The rest must be conjecture. Arabic sources differ over their individual names and perhaps it is a successful measure of the secrecy which they sought for themselves in their age that we know so little about their lives in our own. Like the deserted camp of the beloved in early Arabic poetry, the traces of their passage have become faint and shadowy.

Their written legacy, however, is much more tangible: it comprises a total of fifty-two *Rasā'il* addressed to their associates, each commencing with such characteristic phrases as 'Know, O brother . . .'[3] or, much more rarely, 'Know, O brethren . . .'.[4] It is clear that an extra epistle (*risāla*) was added later for the text contains several assertions that the number of *Rasā'il* is fifty-one.[5] Indeed, the fifty-second and last *Risāla*, which deals with magic and kindred subjects, numbers itself as 51 in one place[6] and refers to only fifty *Rasā'il* having preceded it.[7] Yet, underneath its chapter heading, it is correctly numbered as 52![8] It has been suggested that the obvious predilection for the number fifty-one, which is seventeen multiplied by three, may be linked with the numerical symbolism of the alchemist Jābir b. Ḥayyān, who appears to have flourished in the eighth century AD: the Ikhwān wrote seventeen *Rasā'il* on the natural sciences and seventeen was considered to be a key figure in the Jābirean corpus.[9]

The *Rasā'il* are divided into four main sections, comprising fourteen *Rasā'il* on Mathematical Sciences, seventeen on Natural Sciences, ten on Psychological and Rational Sciences, and eleven on Theological Sciences. A central feature of the whole work is a lengthy debate between man and a variety of representatives of the animal kingdom, which occupies a large part of *Risāla* 22 entitled *On How the Animals and their Kinds are Formed*.[10] Separate from this group of fifty-two is a further *Risāla*, which seems to have been intended as a conclusion, entitled 'The Summary' (*al-Risālat al-Jāmi'a*).[11] The authorship of this has been the subject of some dispute, and, indeed, has been falsely attributed to al-Majrīṭī (died *c.* 1008);[12] but in view of the similar vocabulary, phraseology, and other resemblances it is highly unlikely that its authorship differs from that of the *Rasā'il*.

The Ikhwān discuss the *Jāmi'a* briefly in their list of contents (*Fihrist*)[13] and claim that its purpose is the clarification of the truths which have been alluded to in the other fifty-two *Rasā'il*.[14] The lock of these epistles cannot be opened except by careful study, and it is only after such careful study that one is entitled to read the *Jāmi'a*.[15] The reader is thus led to expect a work of considerable clarity; but the *Jāmi'a* does not, in fact, fulfil its promise nor its final self-designation as 'the crown of the *Rasā'il*'[16] to any large extent, for the work is neither exhaustive nor comprehensive. Much esotericism remains,[17] as well as much repetition. It lacks most of the anecdotes and didactic storytelling of the fifty-two *Rasā'il*, despite the other similarities which have been mentioned, and it is also overladen with Qur'ānic quotation to an oppressive degree not found in these fifty-two.

It seems fairly certain that the *Rasā'il* were the product of meetings (*majālis*) convened by the Brethren for the purpose of philosophical discussion. One author has aptly likened their content to the draft of deliberations by a learned society composed by a well educated secretary,[18] and this could be very close to the truth: the authors of the *Rasā'il* insist that their Brethren hold special meetings at set times, to which none but they are to be admitted, where their secrets and esoteric knowledge can be discussed in peace.[19] Elsewhere it is suggested that such a meeting should take place every twelve days.[20] There is an interesting similarity between these meetings held by the Ikhwān and the meetings attended by the faithful of the Ismā'īlī sect, during the Fāṭimid period in Egypt, which were held twice a week on Mondays and Thursdays for textual reading and study.[21]

It is certainly possible that the *Rasā'il* could be the work of one author only, for there are significant lapses from the usual plural mode of address into the first person singular.[22] This single author has been identified as one of a range of possibilities which includes names as diverse as the previously mentioned al-Majrīṭī, 'Alī (d. 661), Ja'far al-Ṣādiq (*c.* 700–65) and Jābir b. Ḥayyān (*c.* 721–*c.* 815), to cite just a few examples.[23]

Other scholars have preferred to view the *Rasā'il* as a joint undertaking. Thus by the time of the German scholar Flügel in the nineteenth century it was believed that the Ikhwān comprised a group of five thinkers who had formed a secret association in Baṣra and published their *Rasā'il*. This concept of joint authorship goes back to early Muslim sources such as al-Tawḥīdī (d. 1023)[24] and some modern scholars such as S. M. Stern have accepted and reiterated these views.[25] The arguments for and against the various names which have been put forward as the authors of the *Rasā'il* have been discussed frequently elsewhere and will not be repeated here.[26] For even when all the material has been surveyed 'we find ourselves confronted with many contradictory opinions among students of the subject'.[27] In this book the convention is adopted of referring to the authorship in the plural.

An equally vexing problem has been that of fixing the date of composition of the *Rasā'il*. A number of different ways of assessing this from internal evidence have been attempted. L. Massignon, for example, drew attention to the fragments of Arabic and Persian poetry in the text, and the definition of the trigonometrical sine, and suggested that this sort of evidence should be used to discover a date of composition.[28] P. Casanova made use of astronomical data in a similar attempt;[29] but his dating of the writing of the *Rasā'il* of 418–27 AH (1027–35 AD) is rejected by Tibawi, who prefers 338–73 AH (949–83 AD).[30] The disparity in dating between these two authors, whose articles are admittedly separated by forty years, only underlines the difficulties involved in hazarding even an approximate date which will accord with all the internal data of the *Rasā'il*.

As a consequence of the time devoted by scholars to dating and authorship, many equally important problems arising out of the *Rasā'il* have been comparatively neglected or, at best, treated only cursorily. What was the precise relationship of the Ikhwān with the Ismā'īlī movement? How Islamically orthodox are the *Rasā'il*? How have the *Rasā'il* been influenced by Greek and other philosophies? All these questions, and others, posed by A. L. Tibawi, deserve an answer before we can begin to move away from his assessment of the subject of the Ikhwān al-Ṣafā' as a field 'still bristling with a number of question-marks and interspersed with unexplored corners'.[31] Certainly, answers should be found to at least a few of these problems, especially that of the influences, Greek and otherwise, before an attempt is made at a positive personal identification of the authors.

Even the very name of the group, Ikhwān al-Ṣafā', has not been free from controversy: it has led to the story of the ring-dove from Ibn al-Muqaffa''s *Kalīla wa Dimna* assuming a particular importance and significance in the Western history of the *Rasā'il*. According to this story a ring-dove and her companions become caught in a fowler's net. They manage to fly with the net to a friendly rat who nibbles through the net to release them. A crow, who has witnessed and been impressed by the incident, befriends the rat, and later a tortoise and a gazelle join their company. One day the gazelle is caught in a net. His comrades combine to release him, the rat gnawing through the net. The slow tortoise, however, is caught by the huntsman. This time the gazelle acts as a decoy while the rat releases the tortoise and all four animals are saved.[32]

In an important chapter on the human's need for mutual help

or cooperation (*ta'āwun*), the Ikhwān urge the brother to consider the story of the ring-dove in *Kalīla wa Dimna*, and how it was saved from the net, so as to realise the truth of what they have just said about mutual help.[33] Ignaz Goldziher suggested that it was this story of the ring-dove which led the Ikhwān to adopt the name Ikhwān al-Ṣafā'.[34] It is easy to see how this tale, with its emphasis on mutual help and friendship, the double usage of that favourite verb of the Ikhwān, to cooperate (*ta'āwana*),[35] the frequent meeting of the animals to exchange news,[36] and the designation of these animals as Ikhwān al-Ṣafā',[37] could have led Goldziher to regard the tale as the source of the Ikhwān's name. It is clear from the context in *Kalīla wa Dimna* that *ṣafā'* means 'sincerity' rather than 'purity'. Thus the full name of the Ikhwān should be translated as 'Brethren of Sincerity' rather than 'Brethren of Purity', if Goldziher were correct.

His theory might have been plausible if the Ikhwān had described themselves only as Ikhwān al-Ṣafā' without any further additions. But they did not. Their title is frequently elaborated in Mu'tazilite, Ismā'īlī and Ṣūfī terms not found in the story of the ring-dove in *Kalīla wa Dimna*, which Goldziher's theory fails to explain. Examples include: 'Ikhwān al-Ṣafā' and Friends of Loyalty';[38] 'Ikhwān al-Ṣafā' and Friends of Loyalty and People of Justice and Sons of Praise';[39] 'Ikhwān al-Ṣafā' and Friends of Loyalty and People of Praise and Sons of Glory';[40] 'Ikhwān al-Ṣafā' and Friends of Loyalty and People of Justice and Sons of Praise and Lords of the Truths and Possessors of the Meanings';[41] and 'Ikhwān al-Ṣafā' and Noble Friends'.[42] Some of these names are formally cited at the beginning and ending of the *Fihrist* of the *Rasā'il*[43] and might therefore be expected to be official names by which the Ikhwān liked to be known. There is a Mu'tazilite ring to the title 'People of Justice': the Mu'tazila liked to refer to themselves as 'People of Unity and Justice'. The phrase 'Possessors of the Meanings' is a likely reference to the doctrine of *bāṭin* and *ẓāhir*, expounded by the Ismā'īlī sect, in which bodies of scripture like the Qur'ān had an exoteric and an esoteric meaning; while the title 'Lords of the Truths' could clearly have been coined by a Ṣūfī. This is not to say that the Ikhwān embraced Mu'tazilism, Ismā'īlism, or even Ṣūfism fully. Their nomenclature does, however, seem to have been influenced by each of these groups.

The phrase 'Ikhwān al-Ṣafā' ' has been variously translated by orientalists and, indeed, variety has been the one consistent feature of the translations. They have run the gamut from 'Brethren of Purity',[44] 'The Pure Brethren',[45] 'Sincere Brethren',[46] and 'Sincere Friends'[47] in English, to 'die lauteren Brüder',[48] 'die treuen Freunde'[49] and 'die aufrichtigen Brüder und treuen Freunde',[50] in German, back to 'les Frères de la Pureté' in French.[51]

The Ikhwān provide one clue to the real translation of their name in the *Jāmi'a*. Those who are unable to profit from logical proofs and signs are termed 'The Brethren of Turbidity and Misfortune' (*Ikhwān al-Kadar wa 'l-Shaqā'*), who are 'the opposites of Ikhwān al-Ṣafā' and Friends of Loyalty. They are the Friends of Iblīs'.[52] The contrast between 'turbidity' (*al-Kadar*) and 'purity' (*al-Ṣafā'*) is obvious and the latter word could not be translated as 'sincerity' here.

Yet surely the clearest and most frequent clue to the fact that the real translation of 'Ikhwān al-Ṣafā' ' *must* be 'Brethren of Purity' is their emphasis throughout the *Rasā'il* on the need for purity and purification before entering Paradise. The Ikhwān, after all, claimed to be men 'whose minds were pure';[53] since they were specialists on the subject of mental and spiritual purity, they could with justification and insight address others on the same theme:

> When they reach this stage and achieve this position [of exalted knowledge, noble deeds and independence from others in their material needs], we are right to call them Ikhwān al-Ṣafā'. Know, O brother, that the real truth (*ḥaqīqa*) of this name is the special quality actually, not figuratively, inherent in those who are worthy of it. Know, O brother, may the most high God help you, that purity of soul only comes when the soul has reached a state of complete tranquillity in both religious and earthly affairs . . . The man who is not thus cannot be counted as one of the People of Purity (*Ahl al-Ṣafā'*).[54]

Tibawi rather than Goldziher was therefore closer to the truth when he observed that the name 'Ikhwān al-Ṣafā' ' was chosen 'as an imitation of the Ṣūfī tendency to associate their name with *ṣafā* (purity)'.[55]

The treasury of the *Rasā'il* is an extraordinary work, not least because of a number of astonishing statements in it which seem to have been generally accepted until now with hardly a passing comment or expansion, much less detailed examination. It is true that early Islam displayed tolerance towards those whom it called 'The People of the Book' (*Ahl al-Kitāb*), a category which included Christians, Jews and, later, Zoroastrians. This attitude is epitomised in some verses of the Qur'ān, a work which can appear quite favourably disposed towards the People of the Book, when it refrains from castigating their faults: 'And some there are of the People of the Book who believe in God, and what has been sent down unto you, and what has been sent down unto them, men humble to God, not selling the signs of God for a small price; those – their wage is with their Lord . . .'.[56]

Yet the Ikhwān's statements seem to manifest a degree of tolerance and acceptance going far beyond the limited standards of early Islam; if argued to their logical conclusion they would result in heresy (*bid'a*). They appear to be deliberate policy declarations by the Ikhwān and as such deserve to be tested against the content of the rest of the *Rasā'il* to see whether in fact these *Rasā'il* lend some, or indeed any, substance to them, or whether they are isolated remarks with an ephemeral good-will value only.

In these statements the Ikhwān affirm, and indeed urge, a total lack of hostility towards other branches of knowledge and schools of thought (*madhāhib*), and refuse to dissociate themselves from any book written by philosophers and wise men. This does not mean, however, that at the same time they abandon their dependence on the orthodox writings of the prophets, the revelation brought by the latter, and the inspiration which these prophets receive via the angels. Nevertheless, the Ikhwān's own views and particular school of thought embrace all schools of thought and unite all branches of knowledge.[57] These schools of thought and different religions exist as medicines and potions for the treatment of sick souls and – a favourite Platonic theme of the Ikhwān – their salvation from 'the sea of matter and the bondage of nature'.[58] As an aid to such seemingly deliberate eclecticism, the Ikhwān must therefore cultivate a comprehensive mastery of all branches of knowledge in their manifold external and internal aspects.[59]

What are we to make of all this? Does it mean that the Ikhwān adopted a policy of uncritical eclecticism and accepted every religion, dogma and philosophy as equally valid and authoritative? If so, were they 'doctrinal' or only 'textual' eclectics, adding to their own doctrine from those of others, or just using other texts to bolster their own peculiar brand of truth?

This work endeavours to answer some of these questions; there is abundant material throughout the *Rasā'il*, especially in the philosophical and theological sections, on which to base any such quest. It constitutes a fresh approach to the *Rasā'il Ikhwān al-Ṣafā'*, unhampered by considerations of authorship and dating; and, by a critical study of the influences on their thought, it attempts to show what *kind* of philosophers the group of Ikhwān al-Ṣafā' were, rather than to say *who* they were individually.

CHAPTER TWO

The Legacy of Greece 1

PYTHAGORAS

The Islamic conquests of the first centuries after the *hijra* brought the Muslim community a diverse philosophical heritage. Paramount in this was the legacy of Greece. As a result of the increasing contacts of Islam with the Hellenistic world, the Greek luminaries of Pythagoras, Plato and Aristotle began to rise in a new Islamic firmament. As their ideas became better known as a result of the impetus of medical scholarship and the desire for translated texts, they served to influence and inform much of the writing of the intellectuals and philosophers. Among those so influenced were the Ikhwān al-Ṣafā'.

The *Rasā'il* of the Ikhwān are permeated throughout with the spirit of Pythagoras and the Pythagoreans. We know little of Pythagoras himself and he seems to have already become enveloped in legend by the fourth century BC, when Plato and Aristotle wrote. Both seem anxious to avoid mentioning him by name.[1] Yet Aristotle remains our most important source for Pythagoras and early Pythagoreanism. He was certainly familiar with the corpus of doctrine which developed round 'the so-called Pythagoreans',[2] which held that numbers and their properties could explain the whole creation and structure of the universe. Thus it is to him and, to a lesser extent, such hagiographers as the third-century AD Diogenes Laertius and Iamblichus (d. 326), rather than to Pythagoras himself, that reference must be made in the tracing of the Pythagorean elements in the writings of the Ikhwān.

Aristotle noted that the Pythagoreans devoted themselves to the study of mathematics and were, indeed, the first to develop the subject. Their study led them to believe that mathematical principles were at the root of everything. Numbers constituted the first of these principles, and many resemblances were detected between numbers and material and spiritual phenomena; the whole universe was modelled on numbers.[3] These Pythagorean sentiments are evident in the *Rasā'il* in the stress laid by the Ikhwān on the importance of number. Again and again the Ikhwān urge their fellows to acquire a good knowledge of the science of mathematics before proceeding to a study of the three higher sciences of logic, physics and divinity.[4] They declare that the man who has such a knowledge of number with its laws, nature, kinds and properties will obviously be familiar with the number of kinds of created things, together with the reason for their present qualities and why they are neither more nor less than they are.[5] Citing the Pythagorean belief that the nature of created things accords with the nature of number,[6] the Ikhwān proclaim: 'This is the school of thought (*madhhab*) of our Ikhwān.'[7]

As well as sharing the belief that number was a prime principle in the universe and inextricably bound up with its structure, the Ikhwān also resembled the Pythagoreans in attaching a special significance and importance to certain numbers; in this they were by no means unique in their age, as they themselves realised.[8] With the Pythagoreans the number four was sometimes justice because it was the first square number and divided equally; seven was opportunity, for man was 'born after seven months' and reached puberty around the age of fourteen, which is seven multiplied by two. The number five was marriage, being the union of the odd, which was regarded as male, and the even, which was considered female: five is the sum of the first even number, two, and the first odd number, three.[9] Since the number ten was considered to be a perfect number embracing the whole essence of the system of numbers, the Pythagoreans claimed that the moving heavenly bodies added up to ten.[10] Indeed, the number ten achieved a quasi-mystical status by being used in what was called the *Tetraktus* of the Decad. This *Tetraktus* was a group of ten dots which were arranged geometrically in the form of an equilateral triangle (∴∵∴) and it was invoked as their most solemn oath.[11]

However, the number which seems to have been of paramount importance for the Ikhwān was the number four. Pythagoras is supposed to have divided man's life into four quarters, allocating twenty years to boyhood, twenty to youth, twenty to young manhood, and twenty to old age, with these four periods corresponding to the four seasons;[12] but the Ikhwān went far beyond the Pythagoreans in their reverence for this number, and it holds a pre-eminent position of the *Rasā'il* which is by no means confined to the purely mathematical sections of the work. Mathematical science itself is divided into the four parts of arithmetic, represented by Pythagoras and Nicomachus; geometry, represented by Euclid; astronomy, represented by Ptolemy with his *magnum opus*, the *Almagest*; and music.[13] This fourfold division of disciplines, which derived from the Pythagorean school, was, of course, continued in the quadrivium of the Middle Ages.

The Ikhwān arrange numbers in four groups of units, tens, hundreds and thousands, and compare them with the sixteen Pythagorean divisions. There are four ranks above the natural order consisting of Creator, Universal Intellect, Universal Soul and Prime Matter.[14] Particular note is taken of the division of the year into its four traditional seasons; there are four winds and four principal directions of north, south, east and west. Frequent reference is made to the four Empedoclean elements of fire, air, water and earth as well as the four natures of heat, cold, dryness and dampness and the four humours of medieval medicine: yellow bile, black bile, phlegm and blood.[15] The four strings of the lute correspond to the natural order of things[16] while matter is divided into four different kinds.[17] Even good and evil receive a fourfold division.[18] Numerous other examples of groups of four exist in the *Rasā'il*, ranging from the varieties of ignorance[19] and the qualities of the soul to believers in the Qur'ān[20] and the kinds of created things.[21]

The reasons for the emphasis on the number four throughout the *Rasā'il* are less clear than those for the emphasis of other symbolists, for example on the numbers nine, twelve, seven and twenty-eight which were equal to the number of spheres, zodiacal divisions, planets and lunar mansions and which were of major significance in the cosmologies and religions of the Babylonians, Hindus, and Egyptians as well as the Pythagoreans.[22] The reason proffered by the Ikhwān is that the Creator made most things in groups of four and that natural matters are arranged in fours principally to correspond to, or harmonise with, the four spiritual principles which rank above them, consisting of the Creator, the Universal Intellect, the Universal Soul and Prime Matter.[23]

The anthologist John Stobaeus, who lived in the fifth century

AD, noted an identification by Pythagoras of certain numbers with various Olympian gods: for example, the number one was Apollo and the number two was Artemis.[24] However, such absolute identification of number with divine beings does not occur in the *Rasā'il*. Here the Ikhwān prefer to speak of number and God in comparative terms. God is said to have existed before the Universal Intellect in the same way that the number one existed before two.[25] Creatures grow and reach perfection from the emanation of the Creator and His generosity in the same manner that a number increases by the repetition of one. Just as two is the first number to be produced from the repetition of one, so the Universal Intellect is the first created being to emanate from the Being of the Creator. The parallelism is continued, with the number three being compared to the Universal Soul and the number four being compared to Matter, until the thousands are reached, which are compared to the animals. The whole complex symbol is reduced to unity again in the phrase 'The mixture [of all] is like the one',[26] which perhaps reflects the belief that all things are one in matter but many in form.[27] Similarly, elsewhere, the ranks of created beings in the spirit world are said most to resemble the odd numbers while the even, whole and fractional numbers receive other metaphysical parallels.[28]

The Ikhwān stressed that a good knowledge of number was very important as an aid to knowledge about God's unity and they asserted that Pythagoras said that the former led to the latter.[29] Yet with all the emphasis which they placed on number they were able to avoid the cardinal error of the Pythagoreans, described by Aristotle, and make a clear distinction between a number and a thing numbered. Confusing the two, the Pythagoreans believed that not only could the whole universe be considered in terms of number but that it was actually number itself; indeed, 'they defined superficially, and supposed that the essence of a thing is that to which the term under consideration first applies – e.g. as if it were to be thought that "double" and "2" are the same, because 2 is the first number which is double another . . . they hold that things themselves *are* numbers'.[30] However, the Ikhwān demonstrated their awareness of the distinction early in their exposition, stating plainly that the word 'number' indicated a quantity existing in the mind of the numberer whereas the numbered things were actual objects.[31]

The precise contribution of Pythagoras and his followers to the development of musical theory remains in some doubt: J. A. Philip, for example, believes that 'there is no real evidence for the statement often made that Pythagoras "discovered" the numerical relations obtaining in the musical scale'.[32] Nonetheless, the theory of the harmony of the spheres and the idea that the planets and stars produced sounds when in motion was considered to be peculiarly Pythagorean:

> It seems to some thinkers [the Pythagoreans] that bodies so great must inevitably produce a sound by their movement: even bodies on the earth do so, although they are neither so great in bulk nor moving at so high a speed, and as for the sun and the moon, and the stars, so many in number and enormous in size, all moving at a tremendous speed, it is incredible that they should fail to produce a noise of surpassing loudness. Taking this as their hypothesis, and also that the speeds of the stars, judged by their distances, are in the ratios of the musical consonances, they affirm that the sound of the stars as they revolve is concordant.[33]

This notion of a musical firmament was adopted by the Ikhwān, who picturesquely believed that the movements of the stars produced tunes like lutes. Their pure-souled hero Pythagoras is portrayed listening to the nocturnal harmonies resulting from such star movements.[34] On a lower plane, however, music had a more utilitarian function – a charming aspect of early Pythagorean lore was a belief in the cathartic effect of music; it could be relied upon to purge or soothe the emotions. The Syrian Neoplatonist Iamblichus, in his biography of Pythagoras, relates how music was used to influence certain emotions and tells a number of stories which bear witness to its calming effects.[35] These stories have parallels in the *Rasā'il*: a beggar, for example, finds himself exalted above all other musicians because the skill of his playing is able to make his audience laugh, cry and sleep.[36]

The Ikhwān did not, however, endorse everything that was Pythagorean, or characterised as Pythagorean. They rejected, for example, the doctrine of the transmigration of the soul and emphasised the differences which existed between themselves and those who believed in it (*ahl al-tanāsukh* or *aṣḥāb al-tanāsukh*).[37] Nonetheless, the concept of purification which accompanied this Pythagorean doctrine found an echo in the emphasis which the Ikhwān placed on the idea of purity of soul: the obvious example is the name which the group adopted for themselves, Ikhwān al-Ṣafā'. Purity of soul was one of the attributes necessary for admission to Paradise[38] and frequent Qur'ānic quotations back up the Christian beatitude, whose message runs through the *Rasā'il*, that the pure of heart shall see God. The Pythagoreans regarded purity as an essential element in their souls' long journeys of successive incarnations towards ultimate bliss and immortality: sin meant punishment and purification in a lower incarnation. Similarly, the Ikhwān, omitting the idea of transmigration, concluded that purity of soul achieved in this life was an infallible passport to Paradise. The concept has a stark simplicity which many of the Brethren must have found very attractive.

Besides exhibiting concern for the welfare of the soul, the Ikhwān also believed that the body should maintain a correct balance during its 'career' as a prison for the soul, if it wished to be free from sickness. The physician Alcmaeon of Croton, who probably lived early in the fifth century BC, has been regarded by some scholars as not truly Pythagorean.[39] Nevertheless, he probably came into contact with followers of Pythagoras, and Alcmaeon's doctrine of opposites, such as wet and dry, hot and cold, and sweet and bitter, which had to be kept in a harmonious balance for the preservation of health, became characterised as Pythagorean. This doctrine, elaborated into the theory of the four humours, influenced the whole of medieval medicine in both the East and the West, and it is not surprising that the Ikhwān should have shared it. Quoting in an encyclopedic strain from 'one [or some] of the books of the Jewish prophets', the Ikhwān describe how God in creating man put the four humours of black bile, yellow bile, blood and phlegm into his body to regulate it: black bile was made the seat of dryness, yellow bile the seat of heat, while dampness was given the blood as its domain, and coldness phlegm. While each maintained its correct proportions bodily health was preserved; but if one of them became greater than its fellows sickness entered the body.[40]

Such interest in the physical body by the basically ascetic Ikhwān should not be considered strange. They regarded the human being as the most perfect and complete of all living things. Man contained within his body parallels to many of the created phenomena in the world.[41] Since it was impossible for man to know everything about the world in which he lived, God gave him a world in miniature, a microcosm, which was his body.[42] The relationship of the parts of this body to the body itself was like the relationship of some of the planets to the world.[43] The fragile beauty of the concept of the microcosm as elaborated by the Ikhwān pervades a whole epistle.[44] Using a numerical symbolism, which has been described and commented upon elsewhere,[45] the Ikhwān detail the constituent parts of man's frame, together with its growth and function. It is compared to a city and then the analogy is broadened to contain the universe itself in which there are such correspondences as the twelve apertures of the body to the twelve signs of the zodiac, and the nine bodily substances (*jawāhir*) to the nine heavens.[46] The descriptions in this epistle reach a peak of poetic beauty, by the use of symbolism and analogy, which is infrequently encountered in the flat and repetitive style of the *Rasā'il*, and which lends it a mystical quality absent from some of the other epistles which are influenced, for example, by the prosaic Aristotle.

Any survey of Pythagorean and neo-Pythagorean elements in the *Rasā'il* would not be complete without some reference to the work known as *The Golden Verses*[47] which from late antiquity has frequently been attributed to Pythagoras himself.[48] The adjective 'Golden' is said to derive, without foundation in Greek sources, from Galen (*c.* AD 129–*c.* 199), who is reputed to have been an avid reader of the poem and to have copied it in gold letters.[49] The Arabic translation of the work enjoyed great popularity under the title *The Golden Epistle* (*al-Risālat al-Dhahabiyya*), and this is how the Ikhwān themselves generally refer to it.[50] The verses constitute a series of counsels for the initiate in the Pythagorean mysteries and, not surprisingly, suffered a variety of textual changes as they were transmitted.[51] This is well borne out by the four quotations from them in the *Rasā'il*, which each differ slightly in language, meaning and structure.[52] It is clear, however, that all are meant to render, in some fashion, the same Greek lines which have been translated as follows:

> But observe my laws, abstaining from the things
> Which thy soul must fear, distinguishing them well;
> Letting intelligence o'er thy body reign;
> So that, ascending into radiant ether,
> Midst the Immortals, thou shalt be thyself a God.[53]

The Ikhwān's didactic purpose in each quotation is clear: they use *The Golden Epistle* to underline and illustrate particular facets of their teaching such as the immortality of the soul, man's yearning for the hereafter and the bliss of achieving the fourth and highest rank in the hierarchy which they themselves have erected.

PLATO

When we turn to Plato it is difficult to discern much direct influence on the writings of the Ikhwān; for the *Rasā'il* are to a much greater degree Neoplatonic than Platonic. There are only a few references in the *Rasā'il* to works like *The Republic* and the *Phaedo*.[54] The latter is cited in connection with Socrates' death and his final exhortation to sacrifice a cock for him in the temple in fulfilment of a vow.[55] Book Two of *The Republic* is given as the source of the story of Gyges and the magic ring, which is recounted at some length and constitutes the fullest Platonic quotation in the *Rasā'il*.[56] To these items must be added some obvious allusions to the *Crito* dialogue.[57] It is a sparse selection. Nonetheless, a few Platonic notions in the field of philosophy *do* stand out in other parts of the Ikhwān's epistles.

The theme of the body as a hindrance to spiritual perfection and as a prison for the soul is common to both the *Rasā'il* and Plato. The latter believed that man's reason could not function to its absolute capacity until the soul was separated from such physical distractions as pain and pleasure, and even hearing and sight. Likewise he was forced to the conclusion that real truth and pure knowledge could never be attained by the soul while it was diverted by the needs and frivolities of the body.[58] The Ikhwān's outlook was very similar: the view of 'the prophets and their followers and successors and the wise philosophers who share their opinion' that 'these bodies are a prison for souls'[59] is cited with approval and succinctly echoed in the tradition (*ḥadīth*) which they quote: 'The world is the prison of the believer and the Paradise of the unbeliever.'[60] In a powerful simile the soul in the body is likened to a man imprisoned in a lavatory: the faults and blemishes of the body resemble the filth of that lavatory.[61] The theme is pursued in slightly different terms elsewhere: 'Here we are foreign prisoners in the bondage of nature, drowned in the sea of matter . . .'.[62] It is clear that, at best, the body can never have more than a purely functional role as a dwelling-place for the soul. This ambivalent and strained relationship of soul and body is like a house and its inhabitant, a womb and its foetus, a ship crewed by sailors with the shore representing death, and an animal with its rider – a cornucopia, indeed, of lively images employed by the Ikhwān to underline the same Platonic point.[63] Their profound disgust with the world is emphasised at the end of nearly every epistle where the brother is urged to 'turn from the sleep of negligence and the slumber of ignorance [of the body], for the world is a house of delusion and tribulations'. The wise man will never yearn for immortality in such a place of sadness and trial.[64]

Some of the Ikhwān's ideas here about the body may seem to contradict their view of man as the most perfect of all living things, which was mentioned earlier. But the contradiction is more apparent than real for man is being viewed in two different ways: on the one hand he is the brilliant creation of God, comprising body and soul, a veritable microcosm of the whole universe, and therefore must be praised; to do otherwise would be blasphemy. On the other hand, man's human body is responsible for keeping his soul from that same creating God, and for preventing it from enjoying everlasting bliss with Him.

The epistemology of Plato, however, is quite different from that of the Ikhwān. As we have seen, Plato believed that real knowledge could only be achieved in a state of complete separation from the body. But the Ikhwān held that some knowledge of the divine could be acquired here in this world as a means of achieving Paradise. The *Rasā'il* themselves are presented as a corpus of such knowledge and the Ikhwān *rejected* the Platonic belief that learning was just reminiscence and recollection. It is true that a number of scholars, in considering their *Rasā'il*, have made some misleading claims to the contrary and severely limited the role allotted by the Ikhwān to sense impressions in the acquisition of knowledge.[65] But Plato, in his statements about recollection and learning, meant that the soul had had a prior existence in another life before it took up residence in its present body.[66] The Ikhwān did not share this view for they rejected the Pythagorean concept of the transmigration of the soul. Mentioning that many wise men cite the Platonic dictum 'Knowledge is remembrance', the Ikhwān stress that the statement should be interpreted as meaning that the soul is 'potentially knowledgeable' (*'allāma bi 'l-quwwa*) and needs instruction to become 'actually knowledgeable' (*'allāma bi 'l-fi'l*). They explain carefully that the method of instruction should be through the senses, then by the intellect and finally by logical deduction; but without the senses man can know nothing.[67] This was certainly not the view of Plato, who made a firm distinction between the senses and the intellect and considered that the latter was of far greater importance and significance than the former, which were utterly fallible.[68]

The Platonic doctrine of the Forms or 'Ideas' (*ideai*), which occurs so frequently in the Platonic corpus, receives scant attention in the *Rasā'il*, and one of the few references to it is in the nature of a quotation:

> Another said: the various kinds of animals in this world are only pictures and images of those forms and creatures in the world of the spheres and the compass of the heavens, just as the paintings and pictures which appear on the surfaces of walls and ceilings are pictures and images of the forms of these animals made of real flesh. The relationship of beings made of flesh to those creatures with pure essences is like the relationship of these painted, embellished pictures to these flesh and blood animals.[69]

This Platonic exposition is neither commented upon nor pursued and the writers turn at once to another speaker and another theme. The doctrine of Forms is also raised by one of the philosophers of the jinn, who reveals himself as a true Platonist, during the great debate between man and the animals in *Risāla* 22;[70] but again it remains a statement of doctrine thrown to the assembled multitude of men, jinn, and animals and is left undiscussed.

Beyond such brief references – and a few stories attributed to Plato[71] – there is hardly any Platonism in the *Rasā'il*. As we have seen, Socrates and his school are cited in several places, usually to back up a statement by the Ikhwān.[72] Socrates' courageous attitude in the face of certain death, as portrayed by Plato, is greatly admired.[73] Indeed, in one place the description of the deathbed scene is heavily oriented towards the doctrines of the Ikhwān, for Socrates declares that he is going to 'our wise, excellent, noble brethren' (*Ikhwān lanā ḥukamā', fuḍalā', kuramā'*), terms very reminiscent of the hierarchical structure which the Ikhwān erected.[74] The main arguments of the *Crito* dialogue, which portrays Socrates' overriding respect for the rule of law, are summarised in a few lines which conclude: 'He who despises the law will be killed by the law.'[75] It is clear that reverence for Socrates and all that he stood for is one of the two principal Platonic motifs in the *Rasā'il*; the other, of course, being the image of the body as a prison for the soul.

ARISTOTLE

By contrast, Aristotle and Middle Eastern Aristotelianism played a considerable role in the formation of concepts in the *Rasā'il*. It is, of course, a truism that 'Aristotle and Aristotelianism are two different things'[76] and nowhere is this more apparent than in a Middle Eastern context: what starts as basically Aristotelian is likely to end as something that Aristotle would have denied or disowned. A whole host of interpreters, glossators, commentators and exegetes has worked upon him, and many have tried to render him in their own particular image and likeness, according to their own individual beliefs.[77] To claim that Aristotle supported an item of doctrine was, after all, to invoke a powerful authority who could not easily be gainsaid, and many in the East and the West 'jumped on the bandwagon', including the Ikhwān al-Ṣafā': they had no hesitation in producing a story about Muḥammad in which the prophet claims that, had Aristotle lived to know the Islamic message brought by him, the Greek philosopher would have undoubtedly been converted to Islam.[78]

This statement is obviously superficial and slanted, but there is nevertheless clear evidence of Aristotelian influence within the *Rasā'il* themselves. It is true that the principles elaborated in the third and fourth sections (on Psychological and Rational Sciences, and Theological Sciences) are Neoplatonic in inspiration rather than Aristotelian, but nonetheless the Stagirite exercised a considerable sway over the work in the fields of terminology and concepts, and of natural science. Indeed, a number of parallels in title, if not always in content, can be identified between individual *Rasā'il* and the *Corpus Aristotelicum*.[79] Furthermore, the traditional grouping of Aristotle's six logical treatises (*Categories*, *On Interpretation*, *Prior Analytics*, *Posterior Analytics*, *Topics* and *Sophistical Refutations*) into a block under the collective title of *The Instrument* (*Organon*) is paralleled by a similar grouping of treatises in one paragraph of the *Rasā'il*. However, the differences between the two groups will be readily apparent. The Ikhwān wrote:

> The logical sciences are of five kinds: the first is Poetics which is knowledge of the art of poetry; the second is Rhetoric which is knowledge of the art of oratory; the third is Topics which is knowledge of the art of argument; the fourth is Analytics which is knowledge of the art of proof (*al-burhān*); and the fifth is Sophistical Refutation which is knowledge of the art of fallacious argument.[80]

In the following lines, however, the *Categories*, *On Interpretation* and the *Prior Analytics* appear, as well as the *Eisagōgē* of Porphyry (234–*c*. 305) and it becomes clear that the real *Organon* for the Ikhwān comprises the *Categories*, *On Interpretation*, the *Prior* and *Posterior Analytics* and the *Eisagōgē*, since whole epistles are devoted to each of these in the first, mathematical, section of the *Rasā'il*. The initial fivefold division of the logical sciences quoted above is therefore somewhat misleading. The Analytics referred to in this first division are, of course, the *Posterior Analytics*: the Arabic word *al-burhān* is correctly associated by the Ikhwān elsewhere with this treatise and, indeed, they define the object of the *Posterior Analytics* as 'knowledge of how to use sound analogy and true proof (*al-burhān al-ṣaḥīḥ*) in which there is no mistake nor error'.[81] The preoccupation of the Ikhwān with logic and their willingness to exploit the dialectical tools bequeathed by Aristotle together represent one of the most significant legacies from the latter to the *Rasā'il*, and place the Brethren of Purity firmly in that stream of Islamic philosophers which did not hesitate to use the data provided by reason as well as data deriving from the Qur'ānic revelation, to justify their teachings.

In the field of what is called First Philosophy the Ikhwān employed a number of basic Aristotelian terms and concepts such as substance and accident, matter and form, potentiality and actuality, and the four causes. Aristotle used the word 'substance' (Greek *ousia*) in three principal ways: primary substance was something which could not be said of a subject nor described as being in that subject, for example the individual man or individual cow. Secondary substance was a term used to describe the kind or species to which the primary substances belonged, for example man, cattle.[82] Thirdly, the word 'substance' was used in the *Metaphysics* to denote that which made a thing what it was, to denote its essence.[83] Here, then, it was a question of considering *the* substance (what was vital to the very being of something) rather than *a* substance (an individual or species) as in the first two cases.

The concepts of substance and accidents were fundamental to the metaphysics of the Ikhwān but their treatment of them contained a number of novel elements since the basic concepts, once stated, were developed along Neoplatonic rather than traditional Aristotelian lines. What was Aristotelian, however, was the attempt on the part of the Ikhwān 'to determine substance *qua substance* within a *metaphysica generalis*', as Emil L. Fackenheim puts it. The same author goes on:

> But although the Neoplatonic hierarchy rules the whole philosophy of the *Brethren of Purity* and especially the influence of the *Theology of Aristotle* is felt everywhere, a *general* determination of substance *qua* substance seems not to be made impossible thereby . . . So far at least, there seems to be a simple realistic acceptance of the world in an Aristotelian sense, of a world primarily conceived in terms of substance and accident, rather than in terms of an aprioric emanation-structure.[84]

Thus they instruct their brother:

> Know, O brother, that the scholars have said that all things are of two types, substances and accidents (*jawāhir wa a'rāḍ*), and that all substances are of one kind and self-existent (*qā'ima bi-anfusihā*), while accidents are of nine kinds, present in the substances, and they are attributes (*ṣifāt*) of them. But the Creator may not be described as either accident or substance, for He is their Creator and efficient cause.[85]

The gloss which follows shows that the Ikhwān accepted these concepts put forward by the scholars above but subjected them to their own Neoplatonic standpoint. Every created being, therefore, for the Ikhwān, could be described by the ten classical Aristotelian categories. The position of God Himself, however, remains somewhat anomalous since it is not clear whether He is within or beyond being.[86]

The Ikhwān defined – or, better, described[87] – a substance as something 'self-existent and receptive of attributes (*al-ṣifāt*)'.[88] This description, then, is nearer to Aristotle's usage of the word 'substance' in the *Metaphysics* than the dual primary/secondary usage which occurs in the *Categories* (though the Ikhwān seem to have been aware of this latter distinction[89]). The phraseology in their description of substance may differ somewhat from that of Aristotle but the dependence on him in its formulation is clear evidence of the Stagirite's grip on their philosophy. The borrowing from Aristotle, however, ends here – at least, as far as substance is concerned. It was the peculiar difficulty and bold feature of the *Rasā'il* that they sought to integrate their substance/accidents world view with a much larger Neoplatonic hierarchy while also considering substance in terms of matter and form.[90] This development will be illustrated in the next chapter.

Despite their Neoplatonic metamorphosis at the hands of the Ikhwān, the concepts of matter and form, in their simplest descriptions in the *Rasā'il*, retain some Aristotelian characteristics. Aristotle distinguished several kinds of matter but underlying all of them were the same basic ideas that matter continued through change, and had no form in itself though it could receive form; indeed, it could not be found without it. In one place Aristotle observed: 'By matter I mean that which in itself is neither a particular thing nor a quantity nor designated by any of the categories which define Being.'[91] We may compare the Ikhwān's descriptions: matter (*hayūlā*) was 'every substance receptive of form (*ṣūra*)'; form was 'every shape and trace which the substance accepts'.[92] The Ikhwān thus make an equation between matter and substance here and the same equation was made in places by Aristotle: 'That matter is also substance is evident.'[93] Elsewhere, it is true, Aristotle seems to be at pains to separate and distinguish the two words[94] but this only illustrates the fact that such words bear slightly different meanings at various times in the *Metaphysics*. Since it is clear that the Ikhwān depended to a large extent on Aristotle for their definitions, we should not be surprised to find that such definitions, or descriptions, in the *Rasā'il* are similarly varied and sometimes confused.[95]

Any change in matter meant that the old form was lost and a new form was acquired; the basic matter underlying these changes of form was traditionally known as the substrate. Modern scholarship now disputes the idea that Aristotle believed there was 'a single, eternal and completely indeterminate substratum to all physical change, called prime matter'[96] (*prōtē hulē*) but the Ikhwān had no doubt at all that such a concept existed. In harmony with their love of the number four, they described matter in four different ways and, in a manner which was un-Aristotelian, then incorporated the concept of matter in a Neoplatonic hierarchy. The Ikhwān identified (1) the matter of artificial works (*hayūlā 'l-ṣinā'a*), such as the wood used by carpenters, the flour of the bakers, and the earth and water used by builders; (2) the matter of natural objects (*hayūlā 'l-ṭabī'a*), which comprised the four elements of fire, air, water and earth; (3) universal matter (*hayūlā 'l-kull*), which was what they called the Absolute Body (*al-Jism al-Mutlaq*) from which came the stars, the four elements and every other being; and finally (4) Prime Matter (*al-Hayūlā 'l-Ūlā*). As can be seen, these categories are not mutually exclusive.[97] Prime Matter is defined as a 'simple substance (*jawhar basīṭ*)' understood intellectually and not perceived by the senses.[98] All things end in Prime Matter: it is but 'the form of existence' and has neither quality not quantity; 'it is a simple substance with no structure whatsoever which is receptive of all forms'.[99]

Such terms as 'matter' and 'form' are, however, relative: what may be matter to one thing is form to another. This was clearly recognised by the Ikhwān, who illustrate the contrast by taking a dress or shirt (*qamīṣ*) as their example in a passage which also neatly portrays the way in which Prime Matter is fitted into their Neoplatonic hierarchy:

> The dress [or shirt] is one of the artificial and corporeal created objects perceptible by the senses. Its essence (*māhiyyatuhu*) is that it is a form in the cloth and the cloth is matter for it. The essence of the cloth also is that it is a form in the yarn and the yarn is matter for it. The essence of the yarn also is that it is a form in the cotton and the cotton is matter for it. The essence of the cotton also is that it is a form in the plant and the plant is matter for it. The essence of the plant also is that it is a form in the natural bodies which are fire, air, water and earth. Each one of these is also a form in the Absolute Body (*al-Jism al-Mutlaq*) as we explained in the Chapter on Generation and Corruption. The Absolute Body also is a form in Prime Matter as we explained in the Chapter on Matter. Prime Matter is a spiritual

form which emanated from the Universal Soul (*al-Nafs al-Kulliyya*). The Universal Soul also is a spiritual form which emanated from the Universal Intellect (*al-'Aql al-Kullī*) which is the first thing which the Creator created.[100]

The contrast between matter and form may also be studied by examining that between 'the relatively undetermined or unfinished' and the 'determined or finished', making, in fact, a contrast between potentiality and actuality:[101] ' "Actuality" means the presence of the thing, not in the sense which we mean by "potentially". We say that a thing is present potentially as Hermes is present in the wood, or the half-line in the whole, because it can be separated from it.'[102]

These Aristotelian concepts were favourites in the imagery of the Ikhwān and were used for a variety of subjects. The soul, for example, was considered to be potentially (*bi 'l-quwwa*) an angel or a devil and became one or the other in actuality or fact (*bi 'l-fi'l*):

> Know, O brother, that your soul is potentially an angel, and can become one in actuality if you follow the path of the prophets and the masters of the divine laws and implement their counsels mentioned in their books and laid down in the usages of their laws. Your soul is also potentially a devil and will one day actually become a devil if you follow the path of the wicked and the hypocrites.[103]

The minds, or souls, of children were considered to be potentially rational, while those of the mature were actually so; the souls of the rational were potentially knowledgeable while the souls of the learned were knowledgeable in actuality. The souls of the learned had the potential to become philosophers and the souls of philosophers were wise in actuality. Wise men who led good lives were potential angels. Death, which the Ikhwān defined as the separation of the soul from the body, ensured that such men actually became angels. For this reason they characteristically described death as 'a wisdom and a mercy'.[104] Yet the Ikhwān never developed these concepts of potentiality and actuality in any depth; though it may also be fairly noted that even in Aristotle these concepts explain nothing and do not say precisely *why* a thing changes. The Ikhwān's own usage of them is superficial and, at times, almost incantatory, as the above string of examples shows.

The doctrine of the Four Causes – material, formal, efficient and final – was perhaps Aristotle's fullest attempt to provide reasons for what he found in the universe. He cited the bronze from which a statue was made and the silver in a cup as examples of the first. The second cause was the pattern or form which something took, causing it to develop in one way and not another. Thus an apple pip might be expected to produce an apple, rather than an orange tree. By the third cause he indicated the origin or originator of something: a father, for example, was the efficient cause of his child. Lastly, the final cause tried to show the end purpose of something. Aristotle posed the question 'Why does a man walk?' and answered 'To be healthy'. Good health was thus said to be the final cause of walking.[105]

The Ikhwān adopted the same fourfold terminology:

> Know, O brother, that every being under the sphere of the moon has four causes which are all absolutely necessary in the creation of such beings: one of them is a material cause (*'illa hayūlāniyya*); another is a formal cause (*'illa ṣūriyya*); another is an efficient cause (*'illa fā'iliyya*) and another is a final cause (*'illa tamāmiyya*).[106]

A variety of subjects, including meteorology,[107] mineralogy,[108] botany,[109] and carpentry,[110] were dealt with under these headings but the examples of causes in the *Rasā'il*, where the shadows of astrology and Neoplatonism are never far away, sometimes differ radically from Aristotle's more prosaic illustrations. Thus the formal cause of mineral substances is the rotation of the spheres and the movements of the stars round the four elements (*al-arkān*) of fire, air, water and earth.[111] Of the four causes of plants, two are recognisably Aristotelian: the material cause of plants is the above-mentioned four elements while the final cause is the provision of nourishment for animals; but the efficient cause is the powers of the Universal Soul and the formal cause is linked with astral reasons involving a lengthy explanation .[112] The Ikhwān again did not explore this doctrine of the Four Causes in great depth though they recognised that it could lead to dissension, as in the case of the *Duhriyya*,[113] who were thoroughly disliked by the Ikhwān. These were people who believed in the eternity of the universe and they were accused by the Ikhwān of denying its efficient cause out of ignorance.[114]

When they came to consider such concepts as place and void, in the Natural Sciences section of the *Rasā'il*, the Brethren firstly mentioned the popular notion that place (*al-makān*) was a vessel or container (*wi'ā'*) into which something could be put.[115] This notion must have owed something to Aristotle, who observed: 'So it appears that place is a surface-continent that embraces its content after the fashion of a vessel.'[116] But the concept of place as a void or empty space (*al-faḍā'*), into which each body fitted perfectly, indicated a lack of knowledge of the substance of the soul, according to the Ikhwān.[117] Agreeing with Aristotle over the impossibility of having a void,[118] they later argued that place was inextricably bound up with matter; indeed, it was one of the attributes of matter and could not exist apart from it.[119] According to this, any idea of a void, defined as a place in which nothing was put, would have involved a contradiction for the Ikhwān. While they were not always consistent in their treatment of place, their dependence on Aristotle is usually discernible: the Stagirite's definition of place as 'whatever fixed environing surface we take our reckoning from'[120] is echoed in a later formulation by the Ikhwān, in the Psychological and Rational Sciences section of the *Rasā'il*, of place as 'the extremities of the body (*nihāyāt al-jism*)'.[121]

Yet in a number of important respects the philosophy of Aristotle had no influence at all on the Ikhwān. In direct opposition to the view of the Peripatetics, the Ikhwān held that the world was created, or, better, 'invented'.[122] The spiritual aspects of creation – the first emanations such as the Intellect and Universal Soul – were brought into being instantaneously[123] while the rest of the natural phenomena of the world were created gradually over a period of time; the Ikhwān found some indication of the latter in the Qur'ān, which states that God 'created the heavens and the earth in six days'.[124] This verse was elaborated by another which they used to allot a rather wider time span for the creation: 'and surely a day with thy Lord is as a thousand years of your counting'.[125] The emanations played a part in this creation as well: for example, God permitted the Universal Soul a major role in the shaping of the material world.[126] It was a cardinal point of doctrine that it was a finite world and so would one day perish with the cessation of motion.[127] Those whose ignorance led them to believe in an eternal world without a creator would suffer grave injury to their souls; indeed, salvation was only for the believer in a created world.[128] We have already seen how the *Duhriyya* were roundly condemned for their views and there is no doubt that the Ikhwān felt very strongly about this issue.

Another important philosophical divergence lay in the connected question of motion. The universe of the Ikhwān had both Body and Universal Soul.[129] Since all motion in the heavens was due to this Universal Soul,[130] the concept of motion did not have the same importance in the physics of the Ikhwān as it did with the Stagirite, where the question of motion was bound up with that of the First Mover. In any case, it was cosmology rather than physics which interested the Ikhwān in their discussions of motion, time and space. They saw time, for example, as much more than just an Aristotelian measurement of movement. It had both a psychological and an eschatological aspect: psychological because it was a pure form born of the mind, and eschatological because time, like the world itself, was an object of creation. The day which heralded the end of the world would also herald the end of time.[131]

When we turn to the last five *Rasā'il* dealing with the *Organon* in the Mathematical Sciences section, we find that the treatment by the Ikhwān of these logical treatises, despite their enthusiasm for logic, is somewhat rudimentary. As has been mentioned already, the treatises discuss Aristotle's *Categories*, *On Interpretation* (known in the Arabic of the *Rasā'il* as *Bārāmāniyās* from the Greek *Peri Hermēneias*), *Prior Analytics*, and *Posterior Analytics*, and the Neoplatonist Porphyry's *Introduction* or *Eisagōgē*.

The survey of the *Categories* (*al-Maqūlāt al-'Ashr*) begins, as in Aristotle's work, with a consideration of terms. The ten categories listed by the Ikhwān agree with Aristotle's, though discussion of them is considerably telescoped in the work of the former. They comprise: substance (*jawhar*), quantity (*kamm*), quality (*kayf*), relation (*muḍāf*), place (*ayn*), time (*matā*), posture (*naṣba* or *waḍ'*), possession or state (*malaka*), action (*yaf'al*), and passivity (*yanfa'il*).[132] The *Risāla* falls naturally into three major parts of preliminaries, discussion of individual categories, and discussion of such topics as opposites and priority, which parallels the plan of Aristotle's work.[133]

A major point of difference, however, lies in the description of the category of substance. Substance is described, Neoplatonically, as an aspect of form and all substances are stated to be of one kind (*jins*).[134] Thus there is not the division into primary and secondary substances which we find in Aristotle. But the Ikhwān seem to show some awareness of the Aristotelian distinction in that Zayd and 'Amr and Khālid are all identified as individual men partaking in a common humanity which is called a species (*naw'*).[135] Here at least, the Arabic word *naw'* does duty in the Aristotelian sense of secondary substance. The Ikhwān do have a division of substance but it is into spiritual (*rūḥānī*) and corporeal (*jusmānī*) and these divisions are further subdivided, as are the other nine categories.[136]

The five ways in which some things may precede, or be prior to, others agree with Aristotle.[137] However, the Ikhwān do not discuss the kinds of change in their *Risāla* devoted to the Categories, as Aristotle does in his treatise,[138] but do so in another *Risāla* specifically devoted to a consideration of matter, form, movement, time and place.[139] Here it will be found that the six aspects of movement – generation, destruction, increase, diminution, alteration and migration – also accord with Aristotle's list.

The content of the *Risāla* entitled *On the Meaning of Peri Hermēneias* differs little from the Greek treatise. Both seek definitions of names, verbs, sentences, statements, affirmations and negations. The kinds of logic and the relationships which operate in statements are analysed in a much abbreviated form.[140] A similar sort of cursory treatment is found in the two *Rasā'il* devoted to the *Analytics*.[141] In the *Prior Analytics* Aristotle's intention was to demonstrate the syllogism which he regarded as a basic tool for all reasoning, and show how its uses could vary. As with Aristotle, the Ikhwān start by defining terms such as premise (*muqaddima*) and stating the rules necessary for syllogisms with examples of the first, second and third figures. The middle part of this short *Risāla* is occupied with a number of Aristotelian-type syllogisms though they are not stated in such abstract and algebraic terms. It concludes with a tendentious discussion of the importance of logic and logical deduction to philosophy, which is absent from Aristotle's treatise. The *Risāla* also contains a warning by Aristotle against the employment of methods of logic which might lead their proponents into error.[142] It has been noted that much of the terminology at the beginning of the *Prior Analytics* has a mathematical air,[143] with its use of such terms as 'figure' (Greek: *schēma*; Arabic: *shakl*) and 'boundary' (*horos*; *ḥadd*), and this must have given the work a particular appeal to the mathematically inclined Ikhwān.

Like many scientists and philosophers before and after them, the Ikhwān sought to erect some kind of scientific and intellectual framework from which to analyse the phenomena around them and to provide a basis for arriving at the truth. It was clear that man could not, and should not, rely on his senses alone: as Plato so frequently emphasised, these could err wildly. Objects were not, therefore, to be judged by only one sense faculty: more than eyesight, for example, was necessary in the assessment of a mirage.[144] Yet, however the Ikhwān may have viewed Aristotle's second syllogistic treatise, Book A, at least, of the *Posterior Analytics* cannot be described as containing 'a theory of scientific methodology'. It was rather an attempt to show how to present research findings in a coherent fashion; such presentation was the prime function of demonstration.[145] Furthermore, Aristotle noted right at the beginning of his work that instruction and learning rested on knowledge which already existed. The dual nature of this knowledge was succinctly summarised by the Ikhwān in their discussion of the basis of deductive logic. This comprised, very simply, two items of information put in the form of questions: Is it? and What is it?[146]

Their account of the *Posterior Analytics* is more than twice as long as that of the *Prior Analytics*, yet it still falls short of the adequate and, indeed, diverges from its Aristotelian model onto matter and methodologies of its own. In it they concentrate on the intention behind the philosopher's use of logical deduction or syllogism, and identify four methods of thought which past philosophers have adopted in their search for truth: division (*taqsīm*), analysis (*taḥlīl*), definition (*ḥuhūd*) and (logical) demonstration or proof (*burhān*).[147] All these terms have an Aristotelian quality and ring about them but a later division by the Ikhwān, this time of created and spiritual phenomena, does not and is not to be found in the *Posterior Analytics*. Everything, the Ikhwān declare, is ultimately reducible to one of three categories: corporeal and natural (*jusmāniyya ṭabī'iyya*), for example the human body; corporeal and artificial (*jirmāniyya ṣinā'iyya*), for example a city; and spiritual (*nafsāniyya rūḥāniyya*), for example singing.[148] Finally, the discussion of causality in the middle of Book B is reduced in the *Risāla* to little more than a discussion of the fact that effect cannot precede cause.[149]

For the most part, then, the treatment of the *Organon* by the Ikhwān is brief, if not perfunctory, and it is not always faithful to Aristotle's treatises. The surveys of the Ikhwān contribute nothing original to the analysis of logic. They are content to quote received ideas and interweave them occasionally with their own Neoplatonic vision. It has been pointed out that even their use of a sixth term, the individual (*al-shakhṣ*), which is added to Porphyry's five, may very well have been borrowed from al-Kindī (died after 866), the father of Arab philosophy.[150]

A survey of the zoology, botany, mineralogy, meteorology and other natural science sections of the *Rasā'il* is beyond the scope of this book. Yet here too, it should be emphasised, the thought of Aristotle left its mark. Indeed, one scholar has gone so far as to say that 'it was probably Aristotle the natural scientist who had the broadest influence on Arab letters'.[151] A single example must suffice. The Ikhwān classified the animal kingdom in several different ways. One was according to the development of the animals' faculties;[152] another was according to habitat;[153] and a third was a threefold division according to the way in which animals generated their young: there were those which became pregnant and suckled and raised their young; those which mated, and laid and hatched eggs; and, finally, those which did not do any of these things but came into being out of decaying matter and lived for less than a year.[154] The shadow of Aristotle hangs over each of these as is clear from a glance at his *Generation of Animals*: the third division mentioned by the Ikhwān, for example, is a condensed version of the main fivefold classification which appears in that treatise.[155]

The pseudo-Aristotelian writings have a place in the *Rasā'il* as well. Indeed, the confusing eclecticism of the Ikhwān in ranking spurious and genuine works together as of equal authority may be excused only by the fact that they genuinely believed that they were following Aristotle in all cases. Beside quotations from *The Golden Verses* of Pythagoras, and Christ, they also quote from the notorious *Theologia Aristotelis*, a Neoplatonic compilation, falsely attributed to Aristotle, which was, in fact, a résumé of Books IV, V and VI of the *Enneads* of Plotinus (204–70):[156]

> Often have I withdrawn by myself and have doffed my body and laid it aside, and become as if I were naked substance without body, so as to be inside myself, outside all other things. Then do I see within myself such beauty and splendour as I do remain marvelling at and astonished, so that I know that I am one of the parts of the sublime, surpassing, lofty divine world. . . .[157]

The other major spurious Aristotelian text cited in the *Rasā'il* is *The Book of the Apple* (*Risālat al-Tuffāḥa*), which was known in the West by the long-winded Latin title of *Tractatus de pomo et morte incliti principis philosophorum Aristotelis*. This work, which was Arabic in origin and probably composed before AD 900, was written in a Platonic style. It portrays the dying Aristotle discoursing on immortality while occasionally reviving himself with the smell of an apple. The influence of Plato's *Phaedo* on it is unmistakable. The citation of the work by the Ikhwān, with its reference to Aristotle counselling and consoling his disciples on his deathbed, is once again for the purpose of justifying belief in the immortality of the soul.[158]

One is now in a position to attempt an answer to the question which has been posed[159] concerning the depth and accuracy of the Ikhwān's understanding of Greek philosophy, at least with regard to Pythagoras, Plato and Aristotle. Of the three philosophers, they seem to have understood and appreciated Pythagoras the most. His ontological approach to numbers was adapted by the Ikhwān to their own needs and a strongly Pythagorean interest in mathematics and related subjects pervades the whole of the *Rasā'il*. Of pure Platonic philosophy there is little. Plato's mentor Socrates is placed on a pedestal as a wise and good man who knew how to face death bravely, but the questions which his pupil Plato put into his mouth in the various dialogues, such as the existence of Forms like perfect goodness and justice, are hardly raised, much less answered. The Ikhwān had their own questions, didactically posed, dogmatically answered. Only in the field of ethics is much direct Platonic influence perceptible, as where the Brethren's eagerness for learning and knowledge brought them to 'a perfect Socratism where knowledge, the good and virtue are identified with one another'. In the ideal state of the Ikhwān, as in Plato's Republic, the ignorant will be instructed by the wise.[160]

Aristotle stands in the shade of the Neoplatonists. The basic concepts and terminology used by the Ikhwān are his. Their development belongs to the Neoplatonists. Several Aristotelian doctrines are mentioned and, indeed, adopted, but discussion in the manner of, for example, the *Metaphysics* is rare. Aristotelian doctrine seems, on the whole, to have been superficially apprehended. The *Organon* is unoriginally described and the description does not always concur with Aristotle. The acceptance of the Neoplatonic *Theologia Aristotelis* and *The Book of the Apple* as being written by Aristotle himself reflects poorly on the depth of the Ikhwān's knowledge and understanding of Aristotle; though in fairness to the Ikhwān it must be stated that the same mistake was made by many other writers.

The luminaries of Pythagoras, Plato and Aristotle may, however, justly be said to shine in the firmament of the *Rasā'il Ikhwān al-Ṣafā'*. But they shared this firmament with a number of brighter stars which on occasion eclipsed the three Greek sages. The brightest was Neoplatonism.

CHAPTER THREE

The Legacy of Greece 2: Neoplatonism

The reconciliation of a pagan philosophy with the dogmatic theology of any revealed religion poses enormous problems and has evoked different approaches over the ages from those medieval Christian, Byzantine and Islamic scholastics who have attempted the synthesis. A pagan philosophy like Neoplatonism was received differently according to the nature of the religion with which it collided. Thus the medieval Christian world, with its Trinitarian theology, could not have failed to notice, and comment upon, the contrast between Plotinus's three hypostases and the Christian Trinity. Furthermore, different media of transmission gave rise to different versions of the same philosophy. Thus the Muslim world, via the Syriac and Arabic translations of Greek texts, literary forgeries of the same such as the *Theologia*, and the influence of the Alexandrian philosophical school, whose city was conquered by the Arabs in AD 642, received a quite different version of Neoplatonism from that which reached medieval Europe; for its basic strand was Aristotelianism.[1]

This Neoplatonised Aristotelianism is clearly visible in the writings of the Ikhwān al-Ṣafā'. However, before considering the Neoplatonic development of the various Aristotelian concepts which they employed, and their integration with this pagan philosophy, it is profitable to consider first two complementary concepts of paramount importance in Neoplatonism: emanation and hierarchy. Both were adopted by the Ikhwān.

Plotinus, the father of Neoplatonism, has been described as the only philosopher of comparable stature to Plato and Aristotle in the course of later Greek philosophy.[2] He may have been born in Upper Egypt but there is no doubt that he was entirely Greek in his way of thinking and philosophy.[3] He postulated a hierarchy of three hypostases or principles above Matter, comprising The One or The Good, Intelligence or Intellect, and Soul. The first is described as beyond being but the second is said to be both being and the Intellectual-Principle. They are both followed immediately by the Soul.[4] The issue of all things, and especially the second and third hypostases, from The One was described by the Neoplatonists using the image of generation or emanation. Plotinus ingeniously claimed to find his doctrine in Plato[5] and compared the concept of emanation to the ceaseless generation of light by the sun;[6] this seems a highly physical simile but modern scholars have been swift to warn against envisaging light too much in material terms. Plotinus certainly did not.[7]

The Ikhwān followed the Neoplatonists in erecting an emanationist hierarchy of which the first three members corresponded to the Plotinian triad. They noted that things above the natural sphere fell into four ranks. First came the Creator (*al-Bārī*), then the Universal Active Intellect (*al-'Aql al-Kullī al-Fa''āl*), then the Universal Soul (*al-Nafs al-Kulliyya*), and, fourth, Prime Matter (*al-Hayūlā 'l-Ūlā*).[8] The whole scheme of creation and generation resembled the generation of numbers from one:

> Know, O brother, that the first thing which the Creator originated and invented from the light of His unity was a simple essence called the Active Intellect, just as He produced two from one by repetition. Then He created the Universal Celestial Soul from the light of the Intellect, just as He created three by the addition of one to two. Then He created Prime Matter from the movement of the Soul just as He created four by adding one to three.[9]

It will be noted at once that here, with the Ikhwān, Matter is a full member of the emanationist hierarchy whereas with Plotinus it is excluded from his triad of principles, being itself a principle of evil and the cause of any weakness or evil in the soul.[10] However, Plotinus's view that Matter was intrinsically evil was rejected by later Neoplatonists such as Proclus (412–85)[11] and this is, of course, much nearer to the standpoint of the Ikhwān, who never regarded Prime Matter as a principle of evil but rather as 'a positive spiritual principle'.[12]

The Ikhwān, too, employed the image of emanation to describe the relationship between the various members of the hierarchy and they rendered it in Arabic by the word *fayḍ* which means literally 'a pouring forth' or 'flood'. Using a sun simile, which is to some extent like that of Plotinus, they related how the generosity and virtues which were in God emanated (*afāḍa*) from Him 'by the necessity of wisdom (*bi-wājib al-ḥikma*)', in the same fashion that light and brightness emanated from the eye of the sun. The first product of this unbroken emanation (*fayḍ*) was called the Active Intellect, from which emanated, in turn, the Passive Intellect (*al-'Aql al-Munfa'il*) or Universal Soul; from the latter emanated Prime Matter.[13]

Yet the emanation theory of the Ikhwān differs in many respects from that of Plotinus. Not only was it imbued with neo-Pythagorean tendencies, as where the emanation of all things from God was compared to the emanation of all numbers from one, but emanation and creation were not involuntary as in Plotinus's thought, where The One neither willed nor planned the emanations which proceeded from It: the universe came into being, not as the result of some carefully reasoned plan, but out of necessity.[14] We have seen that the Ikhwān use a similar phrase, 'necessity of wisdom', but they make it clear elsewhere in the *Rasā'il* that they considered that the processes of emanation and creation were the results of the Creator's choice and deliberate action. The 'wisdom' referred to is obviously something of which God is in complete control. We are not to think, therefore, that the world exists as a result of a purely natural dispensation or order in which God exercised no choice whatsoever; it does not resemble the sun's light in the atmosphere in this respect.[15]

Furthermore, the full hierarchy of being which the Ikhwān erected was a much more elaborate structure than the simple triad of Plotinus from which the rest of the material world derived or emanated. It comprised nine members or levels of being: the Creator (*al-Bārī*), the Intellect (*al-'Aql*), the Soul (*al-Nafs*), Prime Matter (*al-Hayūlā 'l-Ūlā*), Nature (*al-Ṭabī'a*), the Absolute Body (*al-Jism al-Mutlaq*), the Sphere (*al-Falak*), the Four Elements (*al-Arkān*), and the Beings which live in this world (*al-Muwalladāt*), divided among the mineral, plant and animal kingdoms.[16] Each member was itself composed of a number of things equivalent to the number of the rank which the member held in the above chain of being. Thus the Sphere, which had seventh place in the hierarchy, had seven planets.[17]

Such a hierarchical profusion is slightly reminiscent of the way in which the hypostases were multiplied under Iamblichus (*c.* 250–*c.* 326) and Proclus. The former was responsible for mixing Plotinus's simple triad of The One, the Intellect and the Soul with a whole host of intermediaries, thus elaborating the hierarchy and lending an aura of appalling complexity to later Neoplatonic metaphysics.[18] It is true that this infiltration of other hypostases is not paralleled in the *Rasā'il* in the same manner; but the splitting up of the Plotinian triad by philosophers such as Iamblichus obviously paved the way, and provided the impetus, for other kinds of subdivision, dissection and classification undertaken by later groups like the Ikhwān.

The concept of hierarchy dominates the *Rasā'il*. 'A. 'Awā identifies it as one of the main themes running through the writings of the Ikhwān while Yves Marquet considers a study of their human hierarchy indispensable to a proper understanding of the role of the *Imām*.[19] The concept extended from the chain of being above to many other aspects of life. Perhaps the most obvious example of all is the hierarchy of the Ikhwān, who divided themselves into the four ranks of: (a) craftsmen, who were at least fifteen years of age and were described as 'pious and compassionate (*al-abrār wa 'l-ruḥamā'*)'; (b) political leaders who had attained at least thirty years of age and bore the titles of 'good and excellent (*al-akhyār wa 'l-fuḍalā'*)'; (c) kings, who had attained at least the age of forty and who were called by their fellow brethren 'excellent and noble (*al-fuḍalā' al-kirām*)'; and, last, (d) prophets and philosophers like Abraham, Joseph, Jesus, Muḥammad, Socrates and Pythagoras. Their rank could justly be labelled 'the angelic rank (*al-martabat al-malakiyya*)' and it was not reached before the age of fifty. It was the final rank to which all the Brethren were to aspire.[20]

Other hierarchies and divisions abound in the *Rasā'il*, both animate and inanimate, and it is clear that the Ikhwān viewed the whole world of the human being as a mass of 'grades, classes and circles surrounding each other'.[21] Minerals, plants, animals, men and angels shared in a hierarchy in which the highest member of a lower order was equal to the lowest member of the order above it. Thus the palm, highest member of the plant kingdom by virtue of its possessing some animal characteristics (such as differentiation of sexes), was equal to a member of the animal kingdom and was described, in fact, as an 'animal-plant' (*nabāt ḥayawānī*).[22] Believers in the Qur'ān and the prophetic books were divided according to the whole-hearted nature of their belief, and their knowledge of what they believed in.[23] There were fifteen ranks of soul, of which seven were superior to the human soul and seven were inferior.[24] As for the corporeal side of things, it was divided into the animate and the inanimate: the animate divided into animal and plant, and animal further subdivided into people, birds, fish and similar beings.[25] Sounds were divided into animal and non-animal and both categories were further subdivided.[26] Hell was given its seven traditional ranks of *Jahannam*, *Jaḥīm*, *Saqar*, *Laẓā*, *Huṭma*, *Sa'īr*, and *Hāwiyya*.[27] From all this it is clear that the Ikhwān's interest in classification and hierarchy amounted at times to a positive passion and mania.

Aristotle's categories were also subjected to this kind of formal hierarchisation and division. Thus substance divided first into its corporeal (*jusmānī*) and spiritual (*rūḥānī*) aspects. Corporeal substance then further divided into that which pertained to the celestial sphere (*falakī*) and the natural sphere (*ṭabī'ī*), and so on outwards until a final division into animals born from the womb, those born from an egg, and those born from decayed matter, was reached. Quantity (*kamm*) was similarly divided into the separate (*munfaṣil*) and the linked (*muttaṣil*). The separate divided into number (*'adad*) and movement (*ḥaraka*) and there was further subdivision which ended in the 'units, tens, hundreds and thousands'.[28] It will be readily seen that with such a variety of hierarchies and divisions the Ikhwān had come a long way from the simple majesty of the Plotinian hierarchy composed of The One, the Intellect and the Soul.

It would therefore be wrong to attempt to equate absolutely The One or The Good of Plotinus with the Muslim *Allāh*, or even the Christian God, much less with an ordinary Greek *theos* or *daimōn*,[29] or a Roman *deus*. It is true that all partake in a basic incomparability and majesty. Yet the essence of each differs considerably. The first is unknowable to the extent that a negative theology proclaims that we can only know what The One is not.[30] The second is strictly one in person and sometimes akin to the severe and vengeful Yahweh of the Old Testament, in the admonitory eschatological phrases which He employs in the Qur'ān. The third is Trinitarian in person, and two-natured, possessing a hypostatic union between Father and incarnate Son, while examples of the fourth and fifth are frequently described in a ludicrously anthropomorphic fashion: we note, for example, the machinations of the Gods in the works of Homer and in Virgil's *Aeneid*.

Yet the Ikhwān did attempt a kind of identification between two disparate concepts of deity, between The One of Plotinus and *Allāh* of Islam, though they never directly stated that this was their intention. However, their attempt at grafting *Allāh* onto the top of their metaphysical hierarchy or, to put it another way, their attempt at producing a descending order of being from *Allāh*, involved them in a fundamental dichotomy in their view of God. One scholar has noted that 'most of the contradictions [in the *Rasā'il*] are merely apparent when we go more deeply into the problems'.[31] Here, at least, he is wrong and the inconsistency goes beyond mere detail. It is an outstanding omission in previous studies of the Ikhwān that little or no attention has been paid to their dichotomous view of the divinity.

Sometimes God is successfully described in a Neoplatonic fashion. It is true that, with Plotinus, The One Itself is not the Creator, and should not even be called the First Cause. Any 'predication of action' is utterly precluded by the 'lonely majesty' of the Plotinian concept.[32] Thus creation, as far as The One was concerned, was involuntary. As we have seen, this view was not shared by the Ikhwān. However, Plotinus and the Ikhwān were in agreement on the intermediary roles which the Intellect and the Soul played in the creation of the material world. In the *Rasā'il* the Soul was created through the medium of the Intellect[33] and then God 'created the rest of the living creatures from Matter and arranged them by means of the Intellect and the Soul'.[34] His method was thus to act indirectly with the aid of these intermediaries or with the assistance of other angelic agents such as Nature (*al-Ṭabī'a*).[35] Furthermore, just as the good soul in the *Enneads* longed for a union with The One, like that of two lovers,[36] so every being in the *Rasā'il* was urged to return to God after its sojourn on earth; it should answer the Qur'ānic imperative 'Return unto thy Lord, well-pleased, well-pleasing!'[37] with the emotional formula used during the pilgrimage to Mecca: 'Here I am, oh Lord, here I am! (*Labbayka, Allāhumma, labbayka!*)'[38] The authors of the *Rasā'il* constantly sought to wake their brethren 'from the sleep of negligence and the slumber of ignorance'[39] so that they might successfully rise 'to the Kingdom of Heaven and the realm of the spheres and enter Paradise, the world of the spirits'.[40]

As in the philosophy of Neoplatonism, *Allāh* did not move the world directly but it was moved by the power of the Universal Celestial Soul to whom God had entrusted 'the rotation of the spheres and the movements of the stars and what is under the sphere of the moon'.[41] Thus the Universal Soul operated, as in Plotinus's work, directly on the material world with what it received from the Intellect. God's gifts, for example, were poured firstly onto the Intellect and then received by the Universal Soul which poured them forth, in turn, onto Matter.[42]

At times the Ikhwān make *Allāh* appear almost unknowable in the Plotinian sense in that no attributes may be predicated of Him which might seem to derogate from His divinity and make Him appear in any way human.[43] This raises the related, thorny question of the createdness or otherwise of the Qur'ān, for the Qur'ān was considered to be the speech of God Himself. While orthodox Islam adhered to a belief in the uncreatedness and eternity of the Qur'ān, the philosophical group called the *Mu'tazila*, which was among the first to apply the methodology of Greek dialectic to Islamic thought, espoused a belief in a created Qur'ān. This was adopted by the 'Abbāsid Caliph al-Ma'mūn (813–33) and forcibly imposed for a while by means of an inquisition (*miḥna*).[44]

There are some striking similarities between the theology of the Ikhwān and that of the Mu'tazilite school.[45] However, on the question of the Qur'ān the Ikhwān seem to have attempted to please both parties, orthodox and Mu'tazilite:[46] they distinguished between the actual sounds, words and letters of the Qur'ān, and the ideas or meanings present in the mind of God, and held that the former were created (*makhlūqa*), while the latter were uncreated.[47] An added refinement to this was that God's actual communication of the Qur'ān to the angel Gabriel was considered to be a creation *ex nihilo* (*ibdā'*).[48]

This is all of vital importance in assessing the Ikhwān's view of God and the equation of the 'unknowableness' of the Plotinian One with the incomparability (*tanzīh*)[49] of *Allāh*. For if God is deemed to have no attributes, and if He cannot thus be qualified, He cannot properly be said to have a divine will and the whole notion of divine will becomes superfluous.[50]

Here we may note the contradiction into which the syncretic thought of the Ikhwān has led them: previously it was admitted that God *did* manifest His will in the creation and emanation of the material universe.[51] Now, in an attempt to bolster up the concept of *tanzīh*, this would seem to be denied. As if realising the contradiction, however, the Ikhwān try to wriggle out of it by adopting the expression 'metaphorically' (*'alā sabīl al-majāz*) in the ascription of the divine will.[52] Furthermore, they actually permit anthropomorphic ascriptions to the deity – such as being on a throne in the heavens – *by the common people* (*al-'āmma*) since these help the unscholarly to believe in the very existence of God.[53] Also, since God is the creator of such opposites as existence and non-existence, life and death, and knowledge and ignorance, even the scholars are permitted to say that He is distinguished by the qualities of creation, or immortality or knowledge.[54] 'Awā describes this type of *nomination* – he prefers this French word here to *attribut* – as one of the concessions which the Ikhwān make in order that their rationalist and Mu'tazilite ideas might accord with the data of the Qur'ān.[55] The Neoplatonic aspect of *Allāh* is therefore somewhat confused in the minds of the Ikhwān. It is small wonder, then, that commentators have had difficulty in deciding whether the Brethren considered that God was within or beyond being.[56]

If we turn now to the non-Neoplatonic picture of *Allāh* which the *Rasā'il* also paints, we find that here He is clearly envisaged and portrayed as the God of traditional Islam, acting for and guiding His people directly. He rewards the good and punishes the wicked. Nowhere is it stated that the Intellect or Universal Soul will sit in judgement on the souls of the just or the evil-doers. This is work for God alone:

> The souls of the believers among the saints of God and His good servants will be raised after death to the Kingdom of Heaven and the expanse of the spheres . . . As for the souls of the infidels and the profligate and the evil, they will remain, in their blindness and ignorance, tormented, in pain, grieving and sad, fearful and apprehensive, until Judgement Day.[57]

We have seen that, at times in the *Rasā'il*, God's gifts are poured out indirectly via the emanations.[58] But as the traditional God of Islam and the creator of Adam, the father of all mankind, God has given man many direct gifts such as the means of acquiring knowledge by reading and writing.[59] Indeed, His benefits to man have been countless though the Ikhwān, typically, attempt to classify them, dividing them into external and internal. The external include such things as money, spouse, children and material goods, while the internal are health, good looks, perfect physique, strength and endurance on the one hand, and such features as a good character and an intelligent soul or mind on the other.[60]

The Ikhwān do not, however, specify precisely who the human recipients of all these gifts are to be, but they would certainly have preferred to see them showered on the knowledgeable rather than the ignorant. The description of the gifts is followed by an account of the four states of knowledge into which all men may be divided.[61] Though the Ikhwān claimed to have sent emissaries to every class of society including the artisan,[62] they adopted an intellectually arrogant approach to the common man not possessed of their own wide-ranging learning. Though they identified three classes of beliefs – for the specialist, for the common people and for both – and commended some of the last as best,[63] they nonetheless contrasted in one of their fables the ignorance of the common man with the knowledge and lifestyle of the ascetic scholar.[64] They compared the hands and fingers of the body to domestic servants and workmen, and man's reason to an enthroned king.[65] They spoke in a condescending and sometimes derogatory fashion of the attitudes of ordinary people (*jumhūr al-nās*) to such complex subjects as time and magic.[66] Thus, just as the great philosopher and Ṣūfī al-Ghazālī (1058–1111), in his late treatise *The Restraining of the Common People from the Science of Theology* (*Iljām al-'Awwām 'an 'Ilm al-Kalām*), warned of the dangers in the study of *kalām* by those with too little education, so the Ikhwān warned of the dangers inherent in the study of magic by the common people.

Allāh enables man to carry out His orders[67] and it is He rather than the Universal Intellect or Universal Soul who sends prophets and saints. These constitute, as it were, a race apart for they are humans who have been specially chosen by God as His ambassadors and made intermediaries between the angels and the rest of created men and jinn.[68] Since it is not given to ordinary mortals to speak directly with God, man must receive divine instruction by inspiration or from one of these apostles and messengers who are sent to warn of the last awful Day of Judgement.[69] God Himself is perpetually warning His people through the medium of the Qur'ān, and the *Rasā'il*, with their liberal sprinkling of Qur'ānic quotations, bear ample witness to this. Hypocrites, for example, 'will be in the lowest reach of the Fire'.[70]

The theme of divine guidance is particularly dear to Islam, springing as it does from the Qur'ān, which contains numerous references to it.[71] This idea of God guiding His people is one beloved by the Ikhwān as well, for it is their constant prayer at the end of many of the *Rasā'il* that God may 'grant you and us and all our brothers success in doing the right thing, and guide you and us and all our brothers along the path of righteousness'.[72] This is certainly very far from the unknowable deity of Neoplatonism. Furthermore, this theme of guidance spills over from the divine to the human: ultimately each man must work out his salvation within the framework of the society in which he lives. Since he cannot achieve this on his own, he must have recourse for guidance and help (*mu'āwana*) to those better instructed and qualified than he, for example the Ikhwān,[73] who are described metaphorically at one point as one soul in several bodies.[74] Each man's soul is, in fact, part of a great kingdom of souls, human, super-human and sub-human, all drawing their power from the same Universal Soul which moves the universe. The Ikhwān identify a similar source of power on the social level: salvation, in their view, may be better achieved through membership of a society in which the concept of mutual help or cooperation (*ta'āwun*) is the principal driving force than in the solitary cave of the anchorite who has shunned all contact with men.

Finally, the God of the *Rasā'il* has a very Islamic unity which is stressed throughout the work and which, strangely enough, the emanations of the Intellect and the Soul do not seem to infringe at all. The Ikhwān claim that their intention, in all that they have written, is the proclamation of the unity of God (*tawḥīd*) and His complete and utter freedom (*tanzīh*) from any of the anthropomorphic elements which the ignorant attribute to Him.[75]

There is, then, an unresolved dichotomy in the Ikhwān's treatment of *Allāh* in the *Rasā'il*: to remain within the pale of Islam their deity had to be endowed with some unmistakably Islamic characteristics such as those just outlined above; to remain at the top of their Neoplatonic hierarchy He also had to be treated in a Neoplatonic fashion. But the Islamic ethos which also pervades the *Rasā'il* prevented the Ikhwān's concept of *Allāh* becoming fully integrated with The One of Plotinus.

However, when we turn to the Ikhwān's treatment of the Intellect and the Universal Soul, we find that these are somewhat closer to the Neoplatonic models. Whereas, in any attempt at synthesising concepts of divinity, The One of Plotinus was bound to clash in several respects with the Islamic *Allāh*, there were no indigenous concepts in Sunnī Islam parallel to an emanated Intellect or Soul. It is true that both are to be found in other branches of Islam such as Ismā'īlī Shī'ism but this was the result of borrowing from a variety of external Neoplatonic sources.

There is a certain duality apparent in the second and third principles of Intellect and Soul in the philosophies of both Plotinus and the Ikhwān. For all the other dualities of matter and form, light and darkness, substance and accident, and the like, of which the material universe is composed, derive ultimately from them.[76] The Intellectual-Principle of Plotinus eternally contemplates The One while 'giving birth' to the Soul which is responsible for the production of all the inferior forms of life in the cosmos. A great torrent of feeling, to use blatently anthropomorphic terms, gushes from the Intellect to The One, and from the Soul to the Intellect. Plotinus describes the latter as eternally striving towards, and eternally attaining, The One which he also calls The Good.[77]

Allāh is similarly an object of desire or longing (*shawq*) in the *Rasā'il*. He is 'The First Beloved (*al-Ma'shūq al-Awwal*)', for whom not only the Intellect and the Soul but all created beings are filled with longing. All creation will ultimately return to Him since He is the source of their very existence, sustenance, immortality and perfection.[78] Such was the longing for God which possessed the Universal Soul that, as a direct result, the *muḥīṭ*, the outermost of the spheres in the Ikhwān's universe, came into being; similarly, just as the Plotinian Intellect eternally contemplates The One, so the Intellect in the *Rasā'il* eternally desires union with *Allāh*.[79]

As might be expected however, the Ikhwān's concept of the Intellect has some features of its own which distinguish it from Plotinus's view of this second principle. Being the first creation of God, it receives all four of the Creator's qualities of existence (*wujūd*), immortality (*baqā'*), completeness (*tamāmiyya*), and perfection (*kamāl*) but it only transmits the first three to the Universal Soul.[80] By any standards the Intellect is a mysterious being and the Ikhwān occasionally speak of it as resembling a veil and a gate.[81] As in Neoplatonic philosophy, its principal activity appears to be the generation of the Universal Soul in relation to which it becomes active in contrast to its passivity towards God.[82]

Of the three Plotinian hypostases, Soul has justly been described as 'the most wide-ranging and various in its activities'.[83] The same was true of the Ikhwān's Universal Soul: though feminine by nature, and also grammatically to distinguish it from the masculine Arabic word for body, *jasad*,[84] it was passive only in its relationship with the Intellect but active as far as everything else was concerned.[85] It was responsible for maintaining and moving the material universe, which it had been instrumental in bringing into being,[86] as well as transmitting those virtues and qualities which it received from the Intellect to this material world.[87]

Plotinus, confusingly, used several divisions of soul in the *Enneads*: in some places there was a twofold division into higher and lower souls.[88] In others soul received one of several threefold – or even multifold – divisions, such as that into reasoning soul, sensitive soul and vegetative soul.[89] In a similar manner, the Ikhwān too distinguished between several kinds of soul. As we have seen, there were fifteen different ranks, arranged like the ranks of numbers, of which seven were superior to the human soul, one was human, and seven ranked below the human soul. The two ranks immediately above the human were termed the ranks of royalty and sacredness respectively while the two immediately below were called the animal and the vegetative.[90] However, it has been emphasised that 'the souls in various species in the world such as the animal and vegetative do not actually signify a plurality of souls but various functions of the single Universal Soul'.[91] In the same way, the two- and threefold divisions of soul in Plotinus constituted different levels or facets of the one Soul which was 'a single living continuum'.[92]

Having examined the concepts of hierarchy and emanation, and compared the three Plotinian hypostases with the first three members of the Ikhwān's hierarchy, we are now in a position to look rather more closely at the Neoplatonic metamorphosis which overtook some of Aristotle's concepts at the hands of the Ikhwān and led to 'truly novel mergings of ideas and attempts at unification'. For when Neoplatonists came to deal with the concepts of substance and accident they frequently tended to neglect or ignore the relationship between the two and to treat substance, or rather substances, purely within the context of their own Neoplatonic hierarchical frameworks.[93]

We have already seen one description of substance by the

Ikhwān as something 'self-existent and receptive of attributes (*al-ṣifāt*)'.[94] However, they had an alternative description in which their analysis of substance led them Neoplatonically to matter and form[95] rather than to the atomism of, for example, al-Bāqillānī (d. 1013), a principle of whose metaphysics was that everything (except God) consisted of indivisible atoms and accidents.[96] The Ikhwān wrote: 'Know that form (*al-ṣūra*) is of two kinds: constituting (*muqawwima*) and completing (*mutammima*). The scholars called constituting forms substances (*jawāhir*) and completing forms accidents (*a'rāḍ*).'[97] They later defined their terms as follows: the constituting form (*al-ṣūrat al-muqawwima*) of something was that which could not be separated from its matter without the thing itself ceasing to exist. Completing form (*al-ṣūrat al-mutammima*), on the other hand, was that which raised the object to the best state which it could attain. But, if it were separated from its matter, the matter did not disappear. They gave as examples of completing form silence and movement: if they were separated from the body, the body did not cease to exist. However, length, breadth and depth were considered to be constituting forms whose removal from matter meant the cessation of the body in question.[98]

The Ikhwān used the same terms in a rather more complicated fashion further on in the *Rasā'il* with a variation on the previously expressed idea that what was form to one thing was matter to another. They again used their favourite image of the dress but this time made a contrast between two types of form, rather than Aristotelian matter and form. Here, in this passage, the words 'substantial' and 'accidental' could easily be replaced by 'necessary' and 'unnecessary' or 'essential' and 'non-essential':

> Know, O brother, that every one of these forms is a constituting form for something, either substantial (*jawhariyya*) to it, and completing for something else, or accidental (*'araḍiyya*) to it. The difference between them is that the substantial constituting form for the thing is that which, if separated from the matter, means that the existence of the thing itself ceases. The accidental completing form is that which, if separated from the matter, does not mean the cessation of existence of that matter, for example sewing is a constituting form for the nature (*dhāt*) of the dress and substantial to it, because by it the cloth becomes a dress. [Sewing is, however,] a completing form to the

cloth and accidental in it because if the sewing were taken away from the cloth, the existence of the dress would cease, but the existence of the cloth would not cease.

The chain of reasoning is continued to a point where it is stated that if the second principle, the Intellect, ceased, then the First Creator, God, would still remain.[99]

Elsewhere, the Ikhwān envisaged substance in yet a third way, relating matter and form to it within the framework of a kind of hierarchy of being: substance is divided into two kinds, corporeal and spiritual. Corporeal substance comprises the celestial and the natural while spiritual substances are divided into matter and form. Form is divided into the separable, for example the soul and the intellect, and the inseparable, for example shapes and colours.[100] This kind of division is repeated many times throughout the *Rasā'il*, and does not occur only with the Aristotelian categories. It is typical of the obsessive desire for order which characterises the writings of the Ikhwān and which led them to multiply hierarchies, and divide up concepts, in a vain attempt at perfectly comprehending and embracing the whole universe of *Allāh*.

Enough has now been said for it to be clear that the Ikhwān looked at the concept of substance in a variety of ways. De Boer's observation that the Encyclopedia of the *Rasā'il* 'does not express itself clearly' on points of substance and accidents is surely a gross understatement.[101] There appears to be little real purpose or clear methodology behind the statement of so many different descriptions of substance, composed so eclectically from both Aristotelian and Neoplatonic sources. Some of Aristotle's concepts are metamorphosed indeed, but the average member of the brotherhood established by the Ikhwān cannot have found such a number of differing definitions helpful in his mission.

Although the Ikhwān dealt formally with four separate treatises from the *Organon* of Aristotle, devoting a whole chapter to each, only one work from the Neoplatonic corpus attracted such attention. This was the *Eisagōgē* (Arabic: *Īsāghūjī*) of Porphyry of Tyre, who was both disciple and editor of the great Plotinus. It was written as an introduction to Aristotelian logic as found in the *Categories*, and dealt with five concepts (species, genus, difference, property and accident) which frequently appeared in Aristotle's works. These five terms are sometimes called 'voices', from the Latin, or 'predicables', since they attempted to classify what might be predicated of a given subject.[102] Porphyry's work had an enormous influence on succeeding generations: the early scholastic Boethius (*c.* 480–*c.* 524) wrote a well-known Latin commentary on the *Eisagōgē*, thereby fostering the argument about universals in the Middle Ages which so exercised the minds of such scholars as the Frenchman Peter Abelard (1079–1142).

Right from the time of al-Kindī, who died some time after AD 866, with whom Arab philosophy may be said to start, Muslim philosophers were familiar with the *Eisagōgē* and, indeed, the work became as cherished in the Islamic world as it had been in the Graeco-Latin West.[103] Porphyry is the only Neoplatonist whose name is mentioned in the *Rasā'il* and, of his corpus, it is only with the *Eisagōgē* that the Ikhwān seem to have been acquainted.[104] Even so, apart from the actual chapter devoted to it, the *Eisagōgē* and its author are mentioned very infrequently[105] when compared, for example, with references to another ancient authority, the Alexandrian astronomer and mathematician Ptolemy, and his work the *Almagest*.[106] In the list of contents at the beginning of the *Rasā'il*, the *Eisagōgē* is described as an aid to learning the difference between logical, linguistic and philosophical speech[107] and later is introduced as follows: 'Porphyry the Tyrian wrote a book which he called *Eisagōgē*, and it is the introduction to the craft of philosophical logic.'[108] The opening of the Ikhwān's chapter dealing with it differs somewhat from that of Porphyry's treatise for the former discusses speech and such items as the reason for the enmity between the owls and the crows.[109] However, the subject matter soon becomes similar as the Ikhwān too discuss the various terms or predicables of Porphyry, showing how they differ from each other, though as usual the description is done in a shortened and simplified manner.

The Ikhwān's most important contribution in their assessment of Porphyry's work was the addition of a sixth term, the individual (*al-shakhṣ*), to the Tyrian master's standard five. They observed that, in an attempt at making thought more precise, philosophers had employed six key terms. Three were used to designate substances (*al-a'yān*) or objects which possessed attributes, while three indicated the attributes (*al-ṣifāt*) themselves. The first group comprised the individual (*al-shakhṣ*), the species (*al-naw'*), and the genus (*al-jins*), while the second was composed of the difference (*al-faṣl*), the property (*al-khāṣṣa*) and the accident (*al-'araḍ*). They defined this extra term of theirs, the individual, as a phrase designating a created being which was quite distinct from any other and which could be perceived by one of the senses, for example this man, this riding animal, this tree, etc.[110]

It is quite possible that the term was borrowed from al-Kindī,[111] who lived through one of the most intellectually vital periods of the 'Abbāsid caliphate and was the only other besides the Ikhwān to espouse a doctrine of six voices or terms in Arabic philosophy.[112] Alternatively, depending on the date of composition which is assigned to the *Rasā'il*, the Ikhwān may have been familiar with *The Keys of the Sciences* (*Mafātīḥ al-'Ulūm*) of al-Khawārizmī (*fl. c.* 975) or at least with his contemporaries who knew this work. In it al-Khawārizmī defined 'the individual', under the heading *Eisagōgē*, as '[a term used] by logicians to designate Zayd and 'Amr and this man and that donkey and horse'.[113] The number-oriented Ikhwān may have added the term, for the sake of symmetry and completeness, to the fivefold list of Porphyry.[114]

In any attempt to assess the importance of the role of Neoplatonism in the *Rasā'il* attention should be paid to the difficulties and problems which both the Neoplatonists and the Ikhwān encountered. It has already been shown that the two groups shared much in the way of doctrine, but the problems with which they wrestled were, perhaps inevitably, dissimilar. Many of Plotinus's doctrines could be developed in opposite ways. Matter, for example, was identified with evil but, since Matter was a product of God, could it be considered as absolutely evil? If The One could not be limited how could It remain at the top of a metaphysical hierarchy since this would imply limitation by making It a member, albeit the chief one, of that hierarchy? These and similar questions to which the sometimes ambiguous thought of Plotinus gave rise were left as a legacy to succeeding generations of Neoplatonists who attempted to systematise and clarify his thought, and justify or rectify his twisting of Platonic texts to suit his own arguments.[115]

However, the problems which the Ikhwān inherited, and to which they tried to provide their own answers, were somewhat different. They were much more interested in such Mu'tazilite issues as the attributes of God and the status of the Qur'ān, free will and predestination, and the role of the Imāmate.[116] Listing examples of beliefs which were injurious to the soul, and thus the source of dispute, the Ikhwān included the beliefs that the world was uncreated, that it had two creators (one good and one bad), that the expected *Imām* was hidden for fear of opposition, that God did not forgive sins and that he put evil-doers in Hell and revived them periodically for fresh torture after their bodies had been burned up.[117]

Yet the final goal towards which the Neoplatonists, the Ikhwān, and, of course, the Ṣūfī mystics strove was remarkably similar. All yearned for union of one kind or another with the deity, and saw the interior life of the soul as a haven of security and dependability in periods of turmoil, stress and change. Plotinus lived during perhaps the most troubled era in the history of the pagan Roman Empire – that which extended from the death of Marcus Aurelius in AD 180 to the advent of Diocletian as emperor in AD 284[118] – and the conflicts with Christianity which followed the conversion of Constantine cannot have added to a feeling of security on the part of the later Neoplatonists. The tenth century AD also witnessed its share of upheavals in the Islamic world such as the Būyid seizure of Baghdād in AD 945; Ṣūfism would have appeared a welcome refuge from both political and sectarian conflict.

It is true that the methodology of the three groups differed. Thus the Ikhwān preached throughout their *Rasā'il* that salvation was to be achieved by purification of the human soul and brotherhood. Such purification could be attained by the pursuit of a Socratic-type wisdom, Christian asceticism and Muslim religious devotion.[119] Abstinence from worldy pleasures was particularly enjoined on the legislator (*wāḍi' al-sharī'a*). With Plotinus, however, purification was achievable only through philosophy.[120] But the goal of union with God was the same for all. For Plotinus it was only mystical union that could finally breach the veil and reveal the true nature of the unknowable One:[121] such union could not be described in words for the vision of The One was beyond all description.[122] Porphyry tells us that his master experienced such a state of mystical union four times during the six-year period in which Porphyry knew Plotinus in Rome, and claims also that a similar single experience happened to himself in his sixty-eighth year.[123]

The Ikhwān do not make any comparable confessions of mystical experience in the *Rasā'il* but their intentions are not the less clear because of that; they seek to 'be near the Merciful One of glory and honour'[124] and manifest mystical tendencies which have much in common with the Ṣūfīs: the ideal man is described as being Ṣūfī in his whole way of life.[125] This pointed spiritual espousal of mysticism by the Ikhwān is emphasised in the hierarchical organisation which they erected, which had much in common with the later Ṣūfī orders. The similarity between a lot of the cosmological content of the Rasā'il and Ṣūfism has been emphasised, as has the Ikhwān's usage of Ṣūfī love symbolism: God, as we have seen, is termed 'The First Beloved',[126] and other Ṣūfī terms, such as Abdāl,[127] are to be found scattered in the text of the Rasā'il, as well as Ṣūfī stories – the chapter devoted to music includes one about a Ṣūfī who dies from his longing to return to God.[128]

Akin to the Ṣūfī element in the Rasā'il, and sometimes difficult to separate from it, is a Hermetic strand. It was the Egyptian God Thoth who became Hellenised under the name Hermes Trismegistus, and Hermes (Hirmis) passed into Arabic in a number of forms, the principal being Enoch (Akhnūkh) and Idrīs. To him and to his successors were attributed a whole corpus of philosophical, magical and scientific works.[129] He is mentioned several times by name in the Rasā'il and given the epithet 'threefold (al-muthallath) in wisdom'.[130] The epistles of the Brethren tell how Hermes, 'who is Idrīs the prophet, peace be upon him', went up to the sphere of Saturn and rotated with it for thirty years until he had witnessed all the states of the sphere. He then returned to earth and taught the people about astrology.[131]

The Ikhwān manifest a deep liking and respect for the Corpus Hermeticum and seem to have plundered it for much astrological, alchemical and antediluvian information; indeed, the end of the Risāla on magic is riddled with a variety of quotations attributed to Hermes himself;[132] the Ikhwān indulge in a rare spasm of precision, as far as these Hermetic writings are concerned, by citing his 'fourth book' as a source of information about the creation of Adam.[133] They laud Hermes, too, as a peacemaker between man and the jinn and, somewhat anachronistically, characterise him as a bearer of Islam and its holy law.[134]

However, perhaps the most potent Hermetic influence discernible on the Rasā'il as a whole is the prominent role allotted to astrology. Indeed, the Ikhwān actually say at one point that it is only by a knowledge of astrology that man can attain Heaven.[135]

The planets and stars are described as 'angels of God'[136] which exercise a profound influence over human destiny, but the reader of the *Rasā'il* is warned that only those deeply versed in the divine and astrological sciences can really understand or know much about this.[137] They were complex sciences, requiring much study, for each star had its own different qualities, characteristics and influences.[138] For example, the man whose ruling planet was Saturn would be unlucky in his worldly affairs.[139] All the periods of man's life were subject to the rule of the stars from the foetal stage onwards.[140] These stars could be used to gain information about a pregnancy and discover the sex of a child, and to find out the whereabouts of a thief and whether an absent person was sick or well.[141] However, the Ikhwān castigated those who used astrology to predict the future, for knowledge of the unseen or unknown (*al-ghayb*) was the preserve of God alone and no good could come to any human being by knowing the future.[142] There were thus permissible and impermissible uses to which the knowledge of astrology could be put.

There were contradictions, too, in their espousal and usage of such an art which were not reconciled in their writings. The Hermetic belief in the ruling influence of the stars, which pervades so much of the *Rasā'il*, was in direct contradiction of the Mu'tazilite concept of free will which the Ikhwān also believed in. In the epistles it was admitted that no one could act without God's assistance but that this assistance was never forced upon man who was free to act, or abstain from action, just as he chose. Thus a man could freely choose to use the power which resided in his tongue to speak or to be silent and, similarly, he could elect to open or close his eyes according to his choice.[143]

Apart from astrology there are a number of lesser Hermetic influences on the *Rasā'il* as well. For example, since the number four was considered sacred to the God Hermes, perhaps it is in the *Corpus Hermeticum*, and eclectic works of antiquarian lore such as the *Saturnalia* of the Neoplatonist Macrobius (*fl. c.* AD 400), rather than elsewhere that the origin of the Ikhwān's enthusiasm for that number should be sought.[144] The question inevitably arises of how such influences were transmitted to the Ikhwān. It seems highly likely that they had direct access to some Hermetic literature since they specified that their list of twenty-eight lunar mansions was drawn from the Hermetic work entitled *al-Asṭīṭās*,[145] and they reproduced, almost literally, the last part of this work dealing with these lunar mansions in their fifty-second and last *Risāla* on magic.[146] Some influence must also have been felt from such pagan astrological groups as the Sabaeans who flourished in Ḥarrān (Northern Mesopotamia), and later in Baghdād, particularly during the ninth and tenth centuries AD.[147] In fact, one scholar has viewed the doctrine of the Ikhwān, in at least some respects, as an extension of Sabaean doctrine.[148]

The Middle East has been a cauldron of diverse and frequently conflicting beliefs from time immemorial, and it is now clear that the Brethren of Purity were open to influence by many of the Greek sages' doctrines which bubbled subversively in that cauldron. They took much from Pythagoras and Aristotle and even more from Plotinus; indeed, it has rightly been remarked that the pages of the *Rasā'il* are permeated with the Neoplatonist doctrine of emanation.[149] So it should be no surprise that they found Hermes Trismegistus, with whom the lithe figure of the Greek messenger God Hermes had rapidly become identified, and the Hermetic writings, equally attractive. The *Rasā'il* are a veritable mixture of Neoplatonic, Ṣūfī and Hermetic elements. When it is added that such elements were, nonetheless, unable to prevent an Islamic ethos from pervading the work as well, so that some ideas like the role of God and free will were treated both Islamically and Neoplatonically or Hermetically, it will be realised just how distinctive and syncretic was the flavour which the Ikhwān imparted to their *Rasā'il*.

CHAPTER FOUR

The Christian and Judaic Substrate

CHRISTIANITY AND THE *RASĀ'IL*

Judaism, Christianity and Islam may all be termed 'Abrahamic religions' for all three religions acknowledge a common ancestor in Abraham.[1] The Jewish deity referred to Himself in the Old Testament as the God of Abraham, Isaac and Jacob,[2] while Christ, in the New Testament, was at pains to stress that the faith which He brought was compatible with the religion of Abraham.[3] St Paul stressed the same theme when he observed that by belonging to Christ one was automatically an heir of Abraham.[4] Islam in turn had an enormous respect for Abraham and considered the prophet to be part of the very fabric of the religion. He was revered by Muslims as one who had never been a Jew or a Christian, and certainly not an idolator, but was rather a Muslim himself and the builder, moreover, of Islam's most sacred shrine, the *Ka'ba* in Mecca.[5] It was certainly a tradition of which the Ikhwān approved and which they wished the *Rasā'il* to reflect: proclaiming that their way of thought was 'the religion [or creed] (*milla*) of our father Abraham',[6] they quoted the Qur'ān and asked their readers: 'Who therefore shrinks from the religion of Abraham, except he be foolish-minded?'[7]

This illustration of how the patriarchal Old Testament figure of Abraham is shared by Islam is just a single example of how profoundly syncretic Islam is, with its many Jewish, Christian and pagan elements. This was particularly obvious at its inception when Muḥammad attempted to accommodate the Jews of Medina by ordering that the direction of prayer (*qibla*) should at first be Jerusalem. Nor did Islam hesitate to borrow from Christianity and a brief glance at the tradition (*ḥadīth*) literature, with its wealth of Christian stories and references, readily bears this out.[8]

It was not only the tradition literature which was so influenced. The full extent of the permeation of the *Rasā'il* by Christian thought and scripture has not been appreciated. It is true that most commentators agree that they contain such elements[9] but there exists no full survey or analysis of them which might provide some indication of their richness and number. It is therefore worthwhile, before evaluating the influence of Christianity on the *Rasā'il*, to try and assess the *accuracy* of the Ikhwān's knowledge of this religion.

The Ikhwān must have had easy access to copies of the New Testament for the brother is advised by them to read the Gospel (*al-Injīl*).[10] Certainly, a number of Arabic versions would have been available by their time; from the eighth century AD the Christians of Syria possessed Arabic translations of the Gospels and there were also Arabic copies of New Testament apocrypha in circulation in addition to the canonical Gospels.[11] The differences in language in the transmission of the same Gospel quotation by the Ikhwān in different parts of the *Rasā'il* may attest to the variety of translated texts which they had at their disposal.

Jesus is casually mentioned many times in the *Rasā'il*, frequently as an example of prophethood in conjunction with, for example, Zachary and John the Baptist[12] or Moses and Abraham.[13] He is generally called the Messiah or Christ (*al-Masīḥ*)[14] or simply Jesus (*'Īsā*),[15] but occasionally Jesus Christ (*'Īsā 'l-Masīḥ*).[16] Once He is alluded to as 'Son of the Father (*Ibn al-Ab*)'[17] but the common Qur'ānic title 'Son of Mary' is absent from the *Rasā'il*. Similarly, the Ikhwān frequently cite the Gospel, usually with the Torah and Qur'ān[18] but occasionally with 'the prophetical books'[19] or the Psalms,[20] as an example of a prophetic, revealed book, thereby underlining the particular respect which Islam always showed towards 'The People of the Book'.

The Christianity in the *Rasā'il*, however, goes far beyond mere casual reference and illustration, and it is clear that the Ikhwān were familiar with a large portion of Christian scripture. It is possible from the data provided in the *Rasā'il* not only to construct an accurate and chronological picture of the life of Christ but also to show that the Ikhwān were conversant with a number of Christian doctrines and the dissensions to which these doctrines sometimes gave rise. Apart from a few aspects, which will be commented upon in the course of the following survey, the life of Christ according to the Ikhwān corresponds to that delineated by the four evangelists in the Gospels.

We may begin with the crude formulation of the incarnation doctrine put into the mouth of an incense-swinging, chanting Syrian Christian at the Debate of the Animals: 'Praise be to God who made the body (*jasad*) of the humanity (*al-nāsūt*) from the Virgin Mary, and joined the substance (*jawhar*) of the divinity (*al-lāhūt*) to it, and confirmed him with the Holy Spirit (*Rūḥ al-Qudus*). . . .'[21] The reference to the two natures is interesting and there seems little doubt that the Ikhwān were aware of the Christological controversies between the Nestorians and the Monophysites.[22] The words *nāsūt* and *lāhūt* in the formulation here were Syriac in origin and were used in that language also to denote the humanity and divinity of Christ. Later both were adopted as part of the Arabic Ṣūfī vocabulary.[23] Furthermore, the Ikhwān specifically cited the Nestorians and Monophysites as yet two further examples of sectarian strife.[24] It is possible that the Syrian Christian at the Debate was intended to represent a Nestorian but we are not told. However, the last phrase of his formulation seems to have been inspired by the Qur'ān, where, however, the Holy Spirit whom he mentions is more likely to be a reference to the angel Gabriel, or *Allāh* Himself, rather than the third Person of the Christian Trinity.[25] The Qur'ān may also have been responsible for the references in the *Jāmi'a* to Jesus speaking to the people in the cradle, in another, more astrological, description of the incarnation, though this tradition was common in both Christian and Muslim circles and is to be found in *The Arabic Gospel of the Infancy* as well as in the *Sīra* of Ibn Isḥāq (*c.* 740–*c.* 767) which Ibn Hishām (d. 828 or 833) edited.[26]

We are not told a great deal in the *Rasā'il* about the early life of Christ and in this, of course, these epistles parallel the Gospels. There is a fleeting reference to Him in the Temple of Jerusalem 'at the beginning of His mission' and this is most likely an allusion to the twelve-year-old Jesus being discovered after three days by His frantic parents talking with the scholars in the Temple of Jerusalem. The incident is seen by the Ikhwān to be similar to the way in which Moses began his mission by first informing Aaron and other friends, and the way in which Muḥammad began his by first informing his wife Khadīja and then various friends.[27]

In the *Rasā'il* Christ recruits some of His followers not from humble fishermen but from a company of bleachers whom He meets by the wayside. Yet they obey the call in exactly the same way as the Apostles of the Gospels and, putting on patched garments, accompany Christ on His journeys.[28] He tours the length and breadth of Palestine during His earthly ministry to rescue the people of Israel from 'the death of sin' and He is represented by both evangelists and Ikhwān as a miracle worker.[29] It is a double mission in which physical ills are cured and men are summoned to the Kingdom of God.[30]

After John had been imprisoned by Herod, John's disciples came to Jesus to question Him about the nature of His mission. Christ reassured the confused John through them by referring to His miracles; in a similar way the Ikhwān reassured their audience that it was correct to believe in the immortality of the soul and its blessedness after leaving the body, by citing the ordeal to which Christ subjected His humanity by His death, and the miracle of the resurrection, as indications of the belief of all the prophets in such immortality.[31] Here, of course, Christ's prophethood was viewed quite differently from that of Muḥammad: it was never a tenet of Islam that miracles were a prerequisite, or characteristic, of the latter's mission.[32] It is true that Jesus Himself on occasion refused to work miracles in the Gospels to prove Himself[33] but elsewhere His compassion for the sick and the needy provoked the expected sign. The Qur'ān itself depicts Christ as a miracle worker as, for example, in the miracle of the table. The Apostles test Jesus by asking Him if God is able to send down a table from Heaven from which they can eat. Jesus prays to God and His prayer is heard but God threatens dire punishment for anyone who disbelieves after the miracle. The Qur'ān also refers, a few verses earlier, to Christ's healing the blind and the leprous and raising the dead.[34] So with both Muslims and Christians Jesus is endowed with supernatural powers; indeed, the Christians of Najrān claimed that Christ was divine *because of* His miracles[35] and, of course, it was one of the charges made by medieval Christianity against the prophethood of Muḥammad that it was not confirmed by any.

The Ikhwān recognised that Christ's miracles took place in the soul also: the blindness of the people was spiritual as well as physical and was healed by the application of what the Ikhwān termed 'spiritual substances (*al-jawāhir al-rūḥāniyya*)'. (The Arabic word for 'application' used here (*iktiḥāl*) is particularly vivid since it means basically 'coating the eyelids with kohl'.) Likewise, the sickness of deeply rooted ignorance could be cured by praising God and confirming His oneness.[36] Christ had considerable sympathy and pity for the people to whom He was sent: in the Gospel of St Luke He weeps over the fate which He foresees will overtake Jerusalem in punishment for the obduracy of the Jews,[37] while in the *Rasā'il* He feels compassion for the Jews who profess the religion of Moses but cling only to the externals of its law. They understand neither the Torah nor the prophetical books and only seek the things of this world, ignoring the hereafter.[38] He begins to go round the places frequented by the Jews, warning them, and speaking to them in parables:[39] the wheat will be carried to the granaries but the tares will be burned in the fire.[40]

One of the fullest and most striking examples of Christ's teaching in parables in the *Rasā'il* occurs in His encounter with the company of bleachers. He asks whether they would permit the clothes which they have just washed and bleached to be worn by their owners if the bodies of those owners were soiled with blood, urine and excrement. When they reply that they would not, and that anyone who did so would be a fool, Jesus tells them that they have done just that already. The astonished bleachers ask how this is possible and He tells them that they have cleansed their bodies and whitened their clothes, but their souls are filled with the filth of ignorance and blindness. He urges them to seek the Kingdom of Heaven, and the bleachers leave all and follow him.[41] The incident does not occur in the canonical Gospels but in the apocryphal Gospel of Philip there is a story slightly akin to this in which Jesus enters the dyeworks of Levi and throws seventy-two colours into a vat. When He takes them out, they are completely white and Christ comments that the Son of Man's mission is similar to that of the dyer.[42] However, perhaps the *Rasā'il* episode is much more strongly reminiscent of Jesus's outburst against the scribes and the Pharisees in the Gospels when He scourges them verbally for their hypocrisy and likens them to tombs whose exteriors have been whitewashed and made to appear beautiful while their interiors are full of bones and corruption.[43] Indeed, the Christ of the *Rasā'il* also castigates the bleachers because their very souls are 'soiled with corpses'.[44] The themes of purity and purification were dominant ones in both the Old and New Testaments, just as they were in the *Rasā'il*. It is probable, therefore, that the origins of the Ikhwān's story of the bleachers lie in one of the many biblical references to these themes, such as the Transfiguration scene where Christ's garments become whiter than any earthly fuller could ever bleach them.[45]

Of course, where His audience had already been purified by reading the Torah, prophetical books and wisdom literature, Christ did not need to speak in parables and symbols, and He could speak directly and plainly to the hearts of men.[46] In the *Rasā'il* He is also portrayed speaking to the stones and the trees and, indeed, all that He passes by the wayside; perhaps the closest parallel in the Gospels is when Christ turns to the fig-tree, curses it, and it withers up.[47] Any speech by Christ to non-humans, however, may be regarded as being within the prophetic tradition of Islam. We note, for example, Solomon's speech to the hoopoe bird in the Qur'ān.[48]

The story of Christ's passion, death and resurrection according to the Ikhwān contains a curious mixture of counsels given during the Johannine account of the Last Supper and during Christ's various appearances after the resurrection.[49] In outline, though, it follows the basic pattern of the accounts given by the four evangelists. It begins in traditional fashion with Herod seeking to kill Jesus: 'He was sought by the King of the Jews and their rabble. While the people were assembled around Him, He was assailed and an attempt was made to seize Him. But He avoided them and they were unable to catch Him. . . .'[50] Both the New Testament and the *Rasā'il* extol the obedience of Christ to the will of His Heavenly Father, especially when faced by His passion and death: 'Christ was content with the decree of God and submitted to destiny and surrendered His humanity (*nāsūtahu*) to the Jews. . . .'[51]

Knowing that the appointed time had come, Jesus gathered His disciples to celebrate the Passover. The *Rasā'il* make no mention of this feast here, nor of the breaking of bread and the institution of the Eucharist which took place during the Supper; but the words which Christ speaks bear a marked resemblance to those in the Gospel accounts, though they are occasionally infiltrated with Qur'ānic material: 'When God most high wished to take Him unto Himself, and raise Him to Him, His disciples gathered with Him in Jerusalem in a single room with His companions, and He said: "I am going to My Father and your Father, and I will lay a commission on you before I leave My humanity (*nāsūtī*)." '[52] The first phrase here is clearly drawn from the Qur'ān, where God addresses Jesus thus: 'Jesus, I will take thee to Me and will raise thee to Me.'[53]

So, during the course of the meeting, in the Ikhwān's account, Jesus makes a missionary covenant with His disciples and states that He will have nothing to do with the man who does not accept His commission, a statement reminiscent of His Gospel dictum that the man who did not support Him must necessarily oppose Him.[54] Jesus continues:

> Go to the kings at the ends [of the earth] and inform them from Me of what I have taught you. Summon them to what I have summoned you and neither fear nor stand in awe of them. After separating from My humanity (*nāsūtī*) I will stand in the air on the right hand of the throne of My Father and your Father. I will be with you wherever you go and be your helper, providing you with victory and support, with the permission of My Father.[55]

A characteristically Qur'ānic concept, which was later adopted by the Mu'tazilite group of philosophers, now intrudes into what has been, up to this point, a very Christian series of counsels: 'Go to them and summon them with friendliness; treat them and *command the good and forbid the evil*,[56] until you are killed or crucified or expelled from the land.'[57] The disciples ask for confirmation of the truth of what He has ordered them to do and Christ replies that the confirmation is that He will be the first to do that. What happens next deviates slightly from the account of the evangelists. Jesus is apprehended, not that night in the Garden of Gethsemani, but the following day while teaching the people. Furthermore, it is Herod, rather than Pontius Pilate, who sentences Him to death, though, in fact, neither man is mentioned by name: Herod Antipas is always referred to as 'the King of the Jews (*Malik Banī Isrā'īl*)' – 'The next day He went out and appeared to the people; He began to summon them and warn them until He was seized and brought to the King of the Jews, who ordered Him to be crucified.'[58]

Hereafter the Gospel and *Rasā'il* accounts have a marked similarity:

> So His humanity (*nāsūtuhu*) was crucified and His hands were nailed to the two planks of wood of the cross. He remained

> crucified from the forenoon to the afternoon. He asked for water and was given vinegar to drink, and He was pierced by the lance. Then He was buried in the vicinity of the cross and forty men were set to guard the tomb. All this took place in the presence of His friends and disciples and when they saw what had happened, they were convinced and knew that He had not ordered them to do anything which He Himself had not done. Then they gathered after three days in the place in which He had promised them that He would appear to them and they saw that sign which was between Him and them. The news spread among the Jews that Christ had not been killed so the tomb was opened and His human body (*al-nāsūt*) was not found [there].[59]

The nature of the sign which Jesus manifests to His disciples according to this passage is unclear; it could perhaps be a reference to Christ's apparition on the mountain to which the disciples are directed in Matthew 28:16, or, alternatively, to the revelation of His pierced hands and side, first to the disciples in the absence of Thomas (John 20:20) and later to Thomas as well (John 20:27). The Jews in the Ikhwān's account differ among themselves over the story of Jesus, but the disciples go out, without the benefit of the Paraclete, to north-west Africa, Ethiopia, Rome, Antioch, Persia and India, calling on these countries to accept the teaching of Christ. Some of these missionary journeys, which are merely mentioned by the Ikhwān, find lengthier parallels in the Acts of the Apostles.

It is clear from all this that the Ikhwān had a considerable knowledge of the life of Christ as depicted in the Gospels. There seems, in addition, to be a Nestorian emphasis on His humanity (*nāsūt*), which is frequently mentioned apart from His divinity (*lāhūt*); the Ikhwān stress, as we have seen, that it is Christ's humanity which is given up to the Jews, His humanity from which He will separate, His humanity which is crucified, and His human body which is found to be missing when the tomb is opened.

However, a much more remarkable feature than any latent Nestorianism is that much of what is rejected by orthodox Islamic theology concerning Christ is, in fact, accepted, *at least here*, by the Brethren of Purity. What one Arab author has termed 'the Christian scandal of the Incarnation' is stated, it is true, in the mouth of a Christian.[60] But, as several scholars have noted with surprise, the Ikhwān themselves state that Christ was crucified, died and was buried, and clearly imply that He also rose from the dead.[61] The fact that the stress is on His humanity is unimportant, for the Qur'ānic picture of Jesus, when interpreted by orthodox Islam, is very different:[62] Jesus is born of a virgin, under a palm tree,[63] and His divinity is denied.[64] He is eventually taken up to *Allāh*:[65] '. . . they did not slay him, neither crucified him, only a likeness of that was shown to them (*shubbiha lahum*)'.[66] In other words, traditional Islam teaches that someone else was crucified in Jesus's place. Such a belief obviously precludes any possibility of resurrection from the dead by a crucified Jesus, human or divine.

Elsewhere in the *Rasā'il*, however, the Ikhwān are less than complimentary about Christianity and appear to deny some of what they have already affirmed about it. We have seen a similar contradiction emerge from the Ikhwān's conflicting views about the nature of God and, indeed, a tendency towards such contradiction seems to have been an integral and unavoidable aspect of their syncretic outlook. A further example is the difficulty in reconciling their different definitions, or descriptions, of substance. The Strong Man (*Ṣāḥib al-'Azīma*)[67] at the great Debate of the Animals is in no doubt at all as to the faults of Christianity. He replies at once to the Syrian Christian, who has praised God for the incarnation of Christ, and tells him that he should also have included in his speech the following statement: 'We were infidels and we said: [we believe in] the Third of Three. We worshipped crosses and we ate pork at [our] sacrifice and we told lies and untruths about God.'[68] The reference to the Trinity here is clear but the allegation of eating pork at the sacrifice of the Eucharist is a curious distortion of the doctrine of transubstantiation according to which the basic elements of bread and wine are transformed substantially, as opposed to accidentally, into the body and blood of Christ. It occurs again in the mouth of the pig at the same debate who asserts that 'the [Christian] sons of Byzantium (*abnā' al-Rūm*) vie in eating our flesh in their sacrifices'.[69]

In another place the Ikhwān refer disdainfully to the man who believes that the Jews killed his lord (*rabbahu*), that is to say killed God,[70] and specifically mention that 'among the false views and beliefs which are injurious to the souls of their believers is that of the man who believes that his creator and his God is the Holy Spirit (*Rūḥ al-Qudus*) whom the Jews killed and whose humanity (*nāsūtahu*) they crucified and whose divinity (*lāhūtuhu*) fled on seeing the agony which befell His humanity'.[71]

It may be noted that the description of Heaven which the Ikhwān put into the mouth of Jesus in his conversation with the bleachers is more reminiscent of the physical joys of the Muslim Paradise, which have been described as 'a continuous extrapolation of sensual earthly pleasures',[72] than the Beatific Vision of Christian belief. In the Qur'ānic description, the people of Paradise, dressed in silk, lie on couches with neither heat nor severe cold to trouble them, luxuriating in the shade, and drinking from silver and crystal vessels and cups.[73] In the *Rasā'il* the Ikhwān note that, since Muḥammad came to an illiterate, uneducated people, most of the description of Paradise in the Qur'ān was necessarily of a physical nature to help them to understand and imagine it better.[74] The Jesus of the *Rasā'il* follows the example of the Qur'ān here and describes to the bleachers a Heaven which is almost equally physical in emphasis, though perhaps not so garish, a Heaven free of death, old age, pain, sickness, hunger, thirst, fear, sadness, poverty, need, tiredness, hardship, distress, envy, hatred, boasting and pride; it is a long list which the Ikhwān recite to stress that the ills of the present world will have no place whatsoever in the next. Paradise will be a place of enormous happiness, filled with God's bounty, with angels singing hymns round the throne of God.[75] Elsewhere, however, the Christ of the *Rasā'il* is less physical in His description of Paradise and comes closer to the views held by the Ikhwān on the subject, as He tells His disciples: 'If you follow My example and teaching, you will be with Me tomorrow in the Kingdom of Heaven with My father and your father, and you will see His angels round His throne singing His praises and worshipping Him; you will be there delighting in all the pleasures *without food or drink*.'[76] The Ikhwān reacted against the over-sensual view of Paradise held by some Muslim traditionalists and condemned as false the idea that the people of Paradise had sexual intercourse with virgins whose virginity was then restored, and the belief that the birds of Paradise, once eaten, came to life again and flew away.[77]

Apart from the quotations cited above, which comprise a fairly complete, though brief, survey of the latter part of Christ's life, there remain several other sayings attributed to Christ scattered throughout the *Rasā'il*. These are addressed mainly to the disciples and often find parallels in the New Testament. Several occur more than once with slight differences between each in vocabulary and structure. Sometimes several quotations from differing sections of the New Testament are joined to form one speech by Christ in the *Rasā'il*. Finally, some of the quotation does not occur in the orthodox versions of the New Testament anyway. As we have seen, the Ikhwān had access to the text of the Gospels, which makes it unlikely that every single Christian quotation of theirs was received by hearsay. So how do we account for the differences in transmission? Did they have several different versions of the Gospel text to draw on, including some apocryphal ones? Or were they merely careless in their quotation? The latter would have been uncharacteristic since they show quite a high degree of accuracy in their citation of sacred texts like the Qur'ān, though, admittedly, they would have been much more familiar with this. No definitive answer can be given.

During the well-known visit by the Pharisee Nicodemus to Jesus, at night for fear of being seen by the Jews, Jesus tells him in the course of their conversation that a man will never see God's kingdom without being reborn.[78] The same phrase is put three times into the mouth of the Christ of the *Rasā'il*: 'He who is not born twice will not ascend to the Kingdom of Heaven.'[79] In the two succeeding instances, the verb 'ascend' is replaced by the verbs 'enter' and 'see' respectively.[80] The exegesis of the quotation, of course, differs: Jesus meant rebirth by baptism; the Ikhwān intended it to mean the birth of the soul into a new life at death when, to use their own image, it would find release from its bodily prison. Death was thus a second birth for the soul which endowed it with the ability to travel to the Kingdom of Heaven.[81]

We have already dealt with the missionary covenant made by Jesus with His disciples:

> Go to the kings at the ends [of the earth] and inform them from Me of what I have taught you. Summon them to what I have summoned you and neither fear nor stand in awe of them. After separating from My humanity (*nāsūtī*) I will stand in the air on the right hand of the throne of My Father and your Father. I will be with you wherever you go and be your helper, providing you with victory and support, with the permission of My Father.[82]

A similar amalgam of sayings occurs three more times in the *Rasā'il*, each time in slightly different words, and this underlines the importance which the Ikhwān attached to this kind of covenant.[83] They too claimed to have sent missionaries out to every stratum of society;[84] the whole concept of mission was a common one in the tenth century AD with its abundance of Ismā'īlī missionaries and the propagation of the Fāṭimid mission (*da'wa*). The covenant formula in the *Rasā'il* appears to have been welded together from a number of verses in the New Testament such as the statement that Jesus is seated at God's right hand, Jesus's promise after the resurrection to remain with His church and His command to preach the Gospel throughout the world.[85] It is interesting that the formula becomes more Islamic as it is repeated: in its last citation in the *Rasā'il*, the phrase 'My Father and your Father' is preceded by the Ṣūfī style epithet 'The Truth (*al-Ḥaqq*)' while the name of God is followed by the traditional formula 'May He be exalted and glorified (*'azza wa jalla*)'.[86]

Some of the sayings attributed to Christ in the *Rasā'il* have no parallel in the Gospels but are taken directly from the Qur'ān. For example, Jesus tells God: 'If Thou chastisest them, they are Thy servants; if Thou forgivest them, Thou art the All-mighty, the All-wise.'[87] This is part of a lengthy reply to a question put to Jesus by God in the Qur'ān which the Ikhwān also use in the *Jāmi'a*: 'Oh Jesus son of Mary, didst thou say unto men, "Take me and my mother as gods, apart from God"?'[88] This question is regarded here by the Ikhwān as giving the lie to those disciples of Jesus who exaggerated and said that *He was a God*, giving Him eschatological titles such as 'Master of the Resurrection (*Ṣāḥib al-Qiyāma*)' and saying that He would be in charge of the reckoning of souls:

> Among them [the disciples] were those who said that He was alive and did not die with His body in which He was crucified and that God raised Him to Heaven after three days, and that He will return to the world after His concealment (*ghaybatihi*) and come to earth to take His revenge on the Jews, and that He will reward souls, and many things of this kind, and that He holds the rank of the seventh of the leaders with whom the Resurrection will commence, and He is the *Mahdī* of the nation.[89]

This passage is a strange mixture of Christian and Shī'ite thought, with its talk of a crucifixion and an ascension on the one hand, and the references to concealment, or absence, resurrection, a seventh leader and a *Mahdī* on the other. The disparity between this account from the *Jāmi'a* and the passion narrative from the main body of the *Rasā'il* which we have previously examined is very marked. The Ikhwān underline their disapproval of the disciples' ideas in the *Jāmi'a* by citing the Qur'ānic Jesus's reply to God's question, 'Didst thou say unto men, "Take me and my mother as gods, apart from God"?' Jesus replies: 'To Thee be glory! It is not mine to say what I have no right to. If I indeed said it, Thou knowest it, knowing what is within my soul, and I know not what is within Thy soul; Thou knowest the things unseen.'[90] The sentiments which the Ikhwān condemn are clearly much more explicit in their attribution of divinity to Jesus and so the condemnation is hardly surprising. Its sweeping nature does, however, tend to undermine, if not contradict, some of what they have previously accepted about Christ in their passion narrative. Here, in the *Jāmi'a*, there seems to be an attempt to play down the role of Jesus and He and His message are elsewhere likened, in a striking simile, to a lump of flesh, or embryo (*muḍgha*), for which Muḥammad later provided the bones.[91]

At one point the Ikhwān make a basic mistake in assuming that information contained in the Qur'ān about Jesus is automatically contained in the Gospels. They write:

> Christ, peace be upon Him, *said in the Gospel*: 'Who will be my helpers unto God?' The Apostles said, 'We will be helpers of God.' So He said: 'Be prepared to be killed and crucified if you wish to help Me and be with Me in the kingdom of Heaven with My Father and your Father. Otherwise you do not belong to me.'[92]

It is true that this evokes the scene in the New Testament when some of the disciples leave Jesus, and Jesus asks the twelve Apostles whether they will also leave, together with Simon Peter's famous counter-question as to where the apostles should go since their master has the words of eternal life;[93] but the first part of the quotation is taken directly from the Qur'ān and does not appear in the Gospels as the Ikhwān allege.[94] The second part is, of course, more biblical, and reminiscent both of Christ's warning that the man who does not bear his cross and follow Christ is not worthy of Him, as well as the prophecy of the persecution and death which His followers will face.[95]

There are a number of other sayings put into Christ's mouth in the *Rasā'il* which have no obvious parallels in the Gospels and which also differ with repetition. Thus Christ warns His disciples twice not to squander 'the wisdom (*al-ḥikma*)' by giving it to those unworthy of it, nor to wrong those worthy of it by depriving them of 'the wisdom'.[96] This word is often used in the sense of 'spiritual knowledge' in the Qur'ān; it is mentioned beside revealed bodies of scripture such as the Torah and Gospel as well as being described as something brought by the Qur'ānic Jesus.[97] The whole phrase is perhaps closest in spirit to Christ's injunction in The Gospel of St Matthew not to fling pearls before swine.[98] Elsewhere, in a similarly didactic vein, Jesus warns the scholars and jurists that they have squatted on the path leading to the next world and, in consequence, will not reach it; as the Ikhwān stress, learning and culture are *not* guarantees that their possessors will be rightly motivated into seeking the hereafter or that they will use them as aids in achieving it.[99] The real key to Paradise is abstemiousness in this world and Christ commends to His disciples a diet of barley bread and clear water on this earth for the aspirant to eternal life.[100]

Finally, there are quotations and sayings in the *Rasā'il* which have parallels in Christian scripture, as well as the Qur'ān or *ḥadīth* literature. Both Islam and Christianity emphasise, as we have seen, that many people will find admission to Paradise extremely difficult. The rich man in the New Testament will find access so hard that it will be easier for a camel to pass through the eye of a needle.[101] The same is true for the wicked in the *Rasā'il*, which quote the Qur'ān, saying: '. . . the gates of heaven shall not be opened to them, nor shall they enter Paradise until the camel passes through the eye of the needle.'[102] The well-known statement that no human eyes have seen, nor human ears heard, the joys and pleasures awaiting the faithful in Paradise also appears several times in the *Rasā'il* and has a counterpart in the *ḥadīth* literature and a probable origin in the Bible.[103] Rashīd Riḍā (1865–1935), who criticised many of the literal descriptions of Paradise which abounded in Islam, considered this definition of the hereafter to be 'the authentic *ḥadīth par excellence*'.[104] The popularity in the Middle East of the concept of an unimaginable Paradise is attested by the appearance of the phrase in such apocryphal Gospels as that of Saint Thomas.[105]

The foregoing analysis of quotations in the *Rasā'il* drawn from Christian scripture is one way of highlighting the Ikhwān's knowledge of Christianity; another method is to examine some of their references to Christian doctrine. For example, they refer several times to the Trinity, which Islam has always understood polytheistically as meaning three gods rather than three persons in one God. During the Debate of the Animals the Strong Man cites the belief in 'the Third of Three' as one of the erroneous beliefs of Christianity.[106] In this he adheres strictly to the letter of the Qur'ān: 'They are unbelievers who say, "God is the Third of Three." '[107] Elsewhere the Christians are alleged to have a preference for grouping things in threes (*tathlīth*) and it is clear that this association derives from the Christian doctrine of the Trinity.[108]

Considerable emphasis is placed in parts of the *Rasā'il* on the sonship relationship of Christ with His Father; the terminology used indicates that the Ikhwān were well aware of the Christian belief in Christ as the Son of God. We have already seen this in our examination of the missionary covenant made by Jesus with His followers, where He designates 'My Father and your Father' as 'The Truth (*al-Ḥaqq*)';[109] this was a title normally reserved for God alone and, indeed, death was not an uncommon end for anyone who dared to assume such a title in medieval Islam. The mystic al-Ḥallāj was brutally executed in AD 922 for, among other things, proclaiming, 'I am the Truth (*Anā 'l-Ḥaqq*).' In another place, the Jesus of the *Rasā'il* refers to the throne of 'My Lord (*Rabbī*)',[110] another phrase whose usage was confined in Arabic to God alone. A slave, for example, was not supposed to call his master *rabbī*.

Turning to the Holy Spirit (*Rūḥ al-Qudus*), we find that the Ikhwān's ideas about the third person of the Trinity are more confusing. Jesus is described in the Qur'ān as 'a Spirit from Him [God] (*Rūḥ minhu*)' and as 'His Word (*Kalimatuhu*)'[111] and this is echoed by the Ikhwān in the *Jāmi'a*: Jesus is 'the Spirit of God and His Word sent down from the heavenly host to Mary, the greatest lady'.[112] Here there is an identification of Jesus and Spirit in both the Qur'ān and the *Rasā'il*, and a possible reference to the *logos* doctrine enshrined in the first chapter of the Gospel of St John.[113] But elsewhere in the Qur'ān and the *Rasā'il* the identification of *Rūḥ* is not so simple; as we have seen in the Ikhwān's incarnation description put forward by the Syrian Christian, the line mentioning the Holy Spirit derives from a Qur'ānic verse where the reference could very well be to the angel Gabriel or God Himself. The Ikhwān condemn those who believe that their creator and God was the Holy Spirit crucified by the Jews;[114] later they state, '... there is no God but He, the Holy Spirit', identifying God and the Holy Spirit.[115] This Spirit brings inspiration to the prophets and is linked, early in the *Rasā'il*, with the Universal Soul as the mover of all things.[116] The *Jāmi'a* tells us that It will be encountered by the good soul in Paradise.[117]

A Christian synonym for the Holy Spirit, the Paraclete (Arabic: *Fāraqlīṭ*), is also mentioned by the Ikhwān, once in the fifty-two *Rasā'il* and twice in the *Jāmi'a*.[118] The word is rendered as *Baraqlīṭ* and each time given the epithet 'The Greatest (*al-Akbar*)'. It occurs twice in association with the phrase 'The Expected Mahdī (*al-Mahdī al-Muntaẓar*)',[119] who is also termed 'The Seventh (*al-Sābi'*)',[120] and there seems to be an attempt to link the functions of Paraclete and *Mahdī* eschatologically. The editor of the *Jāmi'a*, J. Salībā, believes that the reference is to the Holy Spirit of Christianity.[121] However, many Muslim commentators have tried to interpret John 14:16, and other passages in the New Testament which forecast the coming of the Paraclete, as prophecies of the coming of the Prophet of Islam, Muḥammad. A theory which has now been challenged states that they were able to do this by confusing the similar Greek words *periklutos* (illustrious or praised) and *paraklētos* (Paraclete). Aḥmad was one of the Prophet Muḥammad's names and the word derives from the same root as Muḥammad: it means 'praised' or, strictly speaking, 'more worthy of praise'.[122] Exactly what the Ikhwān intended by their usage of the phrase 'The Greatest Paraclete' is therefore uncertain though it is clear from its various contexts that it has eschatological connotations.

Man's sinfulness is acknowledged throughout the Qur'ān in its denunciation of such sins as polytheism and theft,[123] though abstract discussion of sin is usually avoided. The first sin of Adam is also condemned[124] and there is perhaps a slight reference here to what became the highly developed doctrine of original sin of the Christian Church. It is made clear in the Qur'ān that Adam is severely punished *for his sin*; he is cast down to earth to suffer in due course the penalty of death: 'Therein you shall live, and therein you shall die, and from there you shall be brought forth.'[125] There is a similar theme in St Paul, who emphasises that death as the result of sin is the fruit of one man's actions.[126]

The doctrine of original sin embraces two concepts in Christianity: it refers to the actual sin which Adam committed, and also to the consequential hereditary stain with which all men are born on account of their origin from Adam. Suffering and death followed in the wake of original sin. It is this latter retributional aspect of the doctrine which finds echoes in the *Rasā'il* as well as the Qur'ān. The *wazīr* who instructs his king about the story of Adam and Eve emphasises that their expulsion from Paradise was a punishment for their sin.[127] There is a recognition that the trials and evils of this world result directly from Adam's sin. Salvation is therefore necessary from the plight into which we have fallen 'through the sin of our father Adam (*bi-jināyat abīnā Ādam*)', a frequently repeated motif in one form or another.[128] For the Christian, man has, of course, been saved and redeemed by the death and resurrection of Christ. But for the Ikhwān it is the mutual help which they themselves can give which will save the neophyte and lead him to salvation from his present plight, 'the sea of matter' and the whole corporeal world which threatens to stifle his soul for ever in its embrace.[129]

An assessment of the Ikhwān's knowledge of, and attitude towards, Christianity may now be attempted. Their acquaintance with Christian scripture has already been demonstrated. This was, however, restricted mainly to the New Testament. They show a much slighter degree of familiarity with the Old Testament and the many Old Testament figures found in the *Rasā'il* are drawn mainly from the Qur'ān, as will be seen in the next chapter, or from Judaic sources other than the Old Testament. (The slight Old Testament influence which *is* perceptible will be examined at the end of this chapter.) The Ikhwān's New Testament knowledge betrays at times a Nestorian emphasis on the two natures of Christ and many aspects of the life of Christ, vehemently rejected by orthodox Islam, are accepted by the Ikhwān, at least in one place. They knew, too, the ranks of some of the clergy in the Eastern Christian Churches and describe the interior of a typical Greek church.[130] All this might lead us to suppose that the Ikhwān's knowledge of Christianity was fairly extensive; but there is doctrinal misinterpretation in the *Rasā'il* as well: the Trinity is not properly understood though the Ikhwān could hardly be blamed for this in view of the general Muslim lack of comprehension of what this doctrine entailed. The identity of the Paraclete is unclear and accusations such as the eating of pork at Mass are cited.

Their basic attitude towards Christianity seems to have been one of tolerance. Doctrine might on occasion be confused but we do not find the Ikhwān's writing about Christianity filled with the asperity and hatred to be found, for example, in the polemics of the Baṣran satirist al-Jāḥiẓ (*c.* 776–868/9).[131] Indeed, the reverse is true at times, as where the Ikhwān advise their brother to read the Gospel.[132] This stems, no doubt, partly from the attitude of tolerance epitomised in the Qur'ānic verse of which the Ikhwān quote the beginning: 'Surely they that believe, and those of Jewry, and the Christians, and those Sabaeans, whoso believes in God and the Last Day, and works righteousness – their wage awaits them with their Lord, and no fear shall be on them, neither shall they sorrow.'[133] But, even more, it is the product of the eclecticism which imbues much of the *Rasā'il*.

This attitude of tolerance led the Ikhwān to be influenced by Christianity perhaps more than they were aware: the most important single factor in this was their total acceptance of Christian scripture as a primary source of equal weight with the Qur'ān and the Torah. Support is freely sought from all three bodies of scripture to back up their statements, though, of course, verses from the Qur'ān predominate if actual quotations from each text are counted. They justify their belief in the immortality of the soul by referring to the life of Christ and provide, as we have seen, a biography of His passion. Christ is considered to be a missionary with equal powers to Moses in His ability to summon men and jinn to God.[134] Recitation of a verse of the Gospel has a power equal to one from the Qur'ān or Torah in protecting the unfortunate traveller from the malevolence of the jinn and from going mad in the desert.[135] At the Debate of the Animals the Gospel, together with the Qur'ān and Torah, is cited as a body of scripture propagating the view that the animal world was created for the benefit and service of man.[136]

A vivid streak of asceticism also runs through the *Rasā'il* which finds its true origin in Christianity rather than Islam, though later Islam too had its ascetics and anchorites. The Ikhwān devote a section of one of their *Rasā'il* to the evils which derive from satiety and they praise the qualities of the abstemious man.[137] The brother is urged to preserve a (Mu'tazilite) moderation or mean in all matters of food, drink and movement and to be generous with what he has, sharing money and knowledge, rather like the first Christians of the early church.[138] If he has foreknowledge of some future disaster, he may take suitable prophylactic measures such as fasting, prayer, sacrifice, intercession to God and repentance.[139]

The ideas of asceticism and monasticism found an early place in the history of the Christian Church, and Islam as it spread could not have avoided coming into contact with them. But the monks upon whom Muḥammad at one time looked kindly were later condemned as devourers of the people's wealth[140] and early Islam maintained a considerable aversion to monastic practices. G. Parrinder sums it up very neatly: 'The general Semitic attitude to life has been broadly described as "world-affirming", as against the "world-renouncing" spirit of India and the Far East.'[141] A. Guillaume puts it more strongly: 'Nothing could be further removed from the point of view of the ordinary Arab of the Jāhiliyya or of Islam than asceticism, as the formidable array of hadith condemning it in all its forms clearly testify.'[142] As we have seen, the Muslim Paradise is described in very sensual and physical terms, surely a deliberate inducement from the ever-present hardships of Arabian life to one of comfort and luxury in the hereafter.

The attitude of the Ikhwān then, in applauding the monastic life according to the Christian model (*'alā 'l-manhaj al-Masīḥī*), contrasts with the traditional Muslim aversion to such practices.[143] Indeed, they acknowledge the Christian origins of their own piety or asceticism when they describe their ideal man as Christian in conduct and Syrian (that is, Christian) in piety or asceticism.[144] Any renunciation must, however, be performed joyfully. The Ikhwān clearly do not think much of the Christian monk who states that the path to God is by denial of personal whim or pleasure, and who is so obviously filled with misery because he feels that he can only approach his God by fasting, prayer and suffering.[145] Much more to their liking is the example of the Christian monks who lived ascetic lives in monasteries and cells and bore witness to their belief in the immortality of the soul by the indifference with which they treated their bodies.[146]

JUDAISM AND THE *RASĀ'IL*

If we turn now to the Judaic substrate of the *Rasā'il* we find that the impact of Judaism is rather less than that of Christianity. It is true that the Torah is frequently invoked with the Qur'ān and

Gospel to substantiate the doctrines of the Ikhwān[147] but quotations from the learned rabbis, similar to the quotations of Christ's sayings from the Gospels, are notably absent. The principal repositories of Jewish thought in the *Rasā'il* are the Judaic stories and traditions which the Ikhwān transmit.

The slighter impact of Judaism on the *Rasā'il* may have been due to a more limited knowledge of the religion. Certainly, they knew of the Jewish expectation of the Messiah[148] and they were also aware that Judaism shared Islam's rejection of pork. But this prohibition was wrongly attributed by the spokesman of the pigs at the Debate of the Animals to the enmity between the Jews and the Christians.[149] The Ikhwān's knowledge of the pre-Christian Book of Deuteronomy cannot have been great for they seem unaware of the prohibition against eating pork which is to be found here.[150]

At this Debate of the Animals the Strong Man briefly compliments the Jews on being a source of Greek science in the days of Ptolemy, but it is stressed by the Greek delegate, to whom the Strong Man is talking, that these sciences were not indigenous to Jewry: Solomon's magic arts did not originate with himself but were borrowed from other nations which he conquered.[151] After the Jewish delegate's enthusiastic eulogy of his Creator, the Strong Man seizes the opportunity to stress the bad qualities of the Jews and his view accords with that held by Muḥammad later in his career after the latter's abortive attempts to reconcile Judaism and Islam in Medina. In a virulent indictment, which echoes a Qur'ānic verse, the Jews are accused by the Strong Man of being apes and swine and worshippers of idols (*Ṭāghūt*).[152] The leader of the birds' delegation appears to accuse the Jews, through the 'Irāqī Jew with whom he speaks, of calling God 'the Third of Three', of saying that 'Uzayr (the Ezra of the Bible), as well as Christ, is the Son of God, and saying that God has the form of a young beardless man. However, it is not clear whether the bird is addressing the man generally as a representative of mankind or specifically as a Jew. If the latter is the case then there is an obvious confusion of Christian and Jewish doctrine, for the Jews have never believed in a Trinity nor that Christ was the Son of God.[153] The attribution to the Jews of a belief in Ezra's sonship of God is however, entirely Qur'ānic: 'The Jews say, "Ezra is the Son of God." '[154] This idea finds no confirmation at all in Jewish tradition.

The above views of Judaism are all taken from the Debate of the Animals but they are significant since the speakers in the Debate, whether human, animal or jinn, very often mirror the thought of the Ikhwān themselves. There remain a number of stories and traditions in the *Rasā'il* which have a basically Judaic rather than a Christian or Qur'ānic provenance, culled from such sources as Midrash, Talmud and Haggadah. Some of the Muslim legend concerning, for example, Abraham, such as appears in the Arabic collections of *Stories of the Prophets* (*Qiṣaṣ al-Anbiyā'*), was derived from these sources, and Muslim tradition in turn influenced later Jewish tradition.[155]

The Ikhwān relate, for example, how Esau wrestled with Nimrod's son and gained the magic hunting-coat of Adam which the son of Nimrod wore. This coat was covered in pictures of all kinds of wildlife. By placing his hand on the picture of the animal which he desired, the wearer was able to halt and seize the animal. Esau was successful in taking the coat because he followed his father Jacob's advice and asked Nimrod's son to remove the coat, which gave him his power, before they wrestled; the latter did so and lost the contest.[156] The giant Nimrod himself, and his adherents, appear in the Qur'ān but only in connection with Abraham. The giant is not mentioned specifically by name but he has been identified by Muslim commentators with the man who disputed with Abraham in *Sūra* 2.[157] In the Old Testament, which gives very little information about him, he is described as a great hunter[158] but this body of scripture contains no parallel to the above story. It is in such sources as the Midrash that more information is to be found about Nimrod: he is portrayed as wishing to kill Esau because of the magic coat which Esau already possesses and which causes all the animals to hurry to him.[159] Later Midrash elaborated the story. Thus we find in the eighth-century AD *Chapters of Rabbi Eliezer* (*Pirḳê de Rabbi Eliezer*) that as soon as the animals see Nimrod in this coat they fall before him. So Esau, who is the jealous one this time, kills Nimrod and seizes the magic garment for himself.[160] However, the *Pirḳê* cannot be used here as an *uncontaminated* Jewish source since it is post-Islamic and was influenced in its accounts of Nimrod and Abraham by the Muslim tradition.[161]

It is significant that the Ikhwān specifically state that their account of Ibn al-Namrūd and Esau is taken from the Torah (*al-Tawrāt*) of the Jews and the Christians, written in Hebrew,

Syriac and Arabic.[162] Here they appear to use the Arabic word *Tawrāt* in a wide sense to indicate the Old Testament, or perhaps just the Pentateuch, in its original Hebrew, as well as the same text in the Arabic and Syriac translations possessed by the Christians. If this is correct, then their mistaken assumption that their account of Nimrod's son and Esau occurs in it is conclusive evidence that the Ikhwān were much less familiar with the Old Testament than with the New; this is confirmed by several other mistakes in the *Rasā'il*.

Among the episodes in the life of Nimrod which are noted in the *Rasā'il*[163] is the notorious attempt by the giant to burn the patriarch Abraham to death. The incident is touched upon in the Qur'ān but the story has obvious antecedents in the Jewish tradition as well.[164] The Ikhwān's own accounts include a charming anecdote from the crocodile at the Debate of the Animals to the effect that, while Abraham was in the fire, the frog carried water in its mouth and poured it onto the fire to quench the flames.[165] In another version the authors of the *Rasā'il* relate how the prophet Muḥammad was asked about the religion (*milla*) of Abraham. He responded with the following story: when Abraham was about to be thrown into the fire the angels in Heaven were filled with pity for him. God therefore suggested to Gabriel that the angel should help him if Abraham sought Gabriel's help. Gabriel finds Abraham in the mangonel which will hurl him into the flames and asks him if he needs anything. The patriarch, because of his great trust in God, replies that he does not need Gabriel. God is moved to save Abraham with the Qur'ānic words: 'O fire, be coolness and safety for Abraham!'[166] The story is a common one in Arabic literature and often very close to this account. Gabriel's question to Abraham, and the prophet's reply, for example, are stated in words very similar to the Ikhwān's in the writings of the historians al-Ṭabarī (d. 923) and Ibn al-Athīr (1160–1233).[167] But there is an obvious parallel to all these accounts in the Babylonian Talmud: here, Gabriel asks God to let him go down to cool the flames and deliver Abraham. God replies that it should be He who performs such a deliverance and promises Gabriel that, in recompense, he will later be instrumental in delivering Hananiah, Mishael and Azariah from the furnace of Nebuchadnezzar.[168]

The story of Jacob and Laban in the *Rasā'il* is attributed by the Ikhwān to 'the second book' of the Torah; this is a clear error for the story occurs in Chapter 30 of Genesis, the *first* book of the Pentateuch and the Old Testament as a whole; the word 'Torah' is obviously used here to render one or other of the latter. The Ikhwān narrate how Jacob seeks leave to go to his own country and tricks Laban into giving him a large quantity of livestock by making Laban promise to give him all his speckled sheep and goats and those which are a mixture of black and white. Jacob then causes his herd to conceive such offspring by placing peeled branches by their watering troughs.[169] It is an account which keeps very close to the version in Genesis.

It is followed by another drawn this time from 'the Books of the Annals of the Kings of the Jews', which are obviously the two Books of Samuel in the Old Testament. The Ikhwān, in fact, mention here the famous prophet Samuel who has a book devoted to him, and who is revered for his prophethood by both Christians and Jews. Samuel gives the Jews a king named Saul (called both in the *Rasā'il* and in the Qur'ān *Ṭālūt*), whom God orders to kill the Amalacites. He does so but disobeys God by not killing their livestock as well. Saul is now no longer worthy of kingship. He begins to kill the magicians but finally has recourse to an enchantress himself to conjure up the spirit of the dead Samuel, who foretells Saul's death as a punishment for his disobedience. Saul falls on his spear during the ensuing battle. This account, with its dramatic description of Saul's visit to the enchantress we know as the witch of Endor, agrees in nearly every respect with that which we find in 1 Samuel.[170]

Here then, in the above stories, are two cases where the material in the *Rasā'il does* accord with the data in the Old Testament. More difficult to trace is a possible source for their sub-chapter dealing with the creation of Adam. They claim that their information is taken from 'one [or some] of the books of the Jewish prophets'. However, these books are not specified and the attribution is highly questionable since the description of Adam's creation is, in fact, an undisguised account of the four humours theory.[171] It is thus much more likely that its real origins are in the humoral pathology of the Hippocratic and Galenic corpus than in any Judaic source. Indeed, both these physicians are named in the *Rasā'il*, which contain a number of quotations attributed to Galen.[172] The whole creation narrative also possesses other elements which will be recognised as characteristic of the Ikhwān in much of their writing: there are *four* natures (*ṭabā'i'*) of heat, cold, dryness and dampness; and *four* humours (*akhlāṭ*) of blood, phlegm, black bile and yellow bile. Furthermore, God teaches Adam the science of medicine and how he may keep his body in good health. One cannot fail to see here the contrast between the medical skill thus taught to the first prophet, Adam, and the Ikhwān's belief that all the prophets and philosophers (including, of course, themselves) were sent as doctors to the souls of other men: 'The prophets, peace be upon them, are the doctors of souls and their helpers and deputies. This is the doctrine of our noble brethren.'[173]

The respect manifested by the Ikhwān for Christianity, and epitomised in the equal reverence accorded to the passions of Jesus and Socrates,[174] contrasts strongly with the attitudes of other writers such as al-Jāḥiẓ. The Ikhwān's frequently sympathetic treatment of Christianity, and the influence which this religion had upon them, must have been significant factors for the commentator who observed that 'in their ideal of the higher life, indeed, the Brotherhood of Purity belong to Christianity rather than to Islām'.[175] This treatment also contrasts with that which they themselves gave to Judaism: despite their quotation of Jewish stories, and usage of the Torah as a primary source with the Gospel and Qur'ān, the Jewish faith was dealt with less frequently, and sometimes viewed less sympathetically; we have noted already the accusations levelled against Judaism at the Debate of the Animals though, in fairness, it must be pointed out that criticism of Christianity at the same Debate is by no means absent. But there is no acceptance of Jewish belief in the same way that the Christian belief in the crucifixion of Christ is accepted in one place by the Ikhwān, contrary to orthodox Islamic teaching. The *Rasā'il* also contain a story about a travelling Jew and a Zoroastrian which has a distinctly anti-Semitic flavour. The Zoroastrian, who charitably assumes the mantle of a latter-day 'Good Samaritan' because of the way his religion has raised him, befriends and aids a Jew whose neck has been broken in a fall from the mule which the Jew has earlier tricked out of the Zoroastrian. The self-centred Jew excuses his behaviour by saying that this is how *his* religion has brought *him* up.[176] The Jew thus appears in a very poor light, which contrasts vividly with the admiration in which the Ikhwān held the figure of Christ; indeed, the charitable sentiments and actions of the Zoroastrian in the story would certainly have commended themselves to the founder of Christianity. Of the two religions then, Christianity clearly exercised the stronger hold on the minds of the Ikhwān al-Ṣafā' and had the greater appeal for them.

CHAPTER FIVE

Uses of Literature

THE CLOAK OF THE QUR'ĀN

The *Rasā'il* contain much that would have been unacceptable to Sunnī Islam; the previous chapters provide some indication of the degree to which the Ikhwān drew on non-Islamic sources. Yet they concealed their own identities so skilfully that modern scholarship, as we saw in the introductory chapter, has spilled much ink in trying to trace the members of the group. There is no record in the *Rasā'il* that the Ikhwān themselves ever suffered physical violence or persecution as a result of their writings. Indeed, the fact that they should be able to claim that one of their number had been sent to every group of people, to kings, scholars and workers,[1] and that their epistles, though suspect, should have had a circulation among orthodox Muslims,[2] is a tribute to the way in which they successfully disguised some of the unorthodox implications of their philosophy.

Using a vivid metaphor, they referred to themselves as 'sleepers in the cave of our father Adam'.[3] Much of their doctrine must also have been hidden from the casual or careless reader, and many of the ordinary people. In one place they gave as their reason for hiding their secrets from the people, not fear of earthly rulers nor trouble from the common populace, but a desire to protect their God-given gifts. In support of this they invoked Christ's dictum not to squander 'the wisdom (*al-ḥikma*)' by giving it to those unworthy of it.[4] Yet they were well aware that their teaching might also provoke unrest and so observe in another place that the calamities suffered by the successors of the Prophet Muḥammad were a good reason for the Ikhwān's remaining hidden until the right day came for them to emerge from their cave and wake from their long sleep.[5] To live safely, it was necessary for their doctrines to be cloaked in an orthodox Islamic garb. Since they believed that everything had an internal or esoteric (*bāṭin*) and an external or exoteric (*ẓāhir*) aspect,[6] we may say that the external cloak which they used to disguise – or at least, make less obvious to unfriendly eyes – their internal Neoplatonism and eclectic toleration, was woven from the Qur'ān. This is *not* to say that they did not accept the revealed message of the Qur'ān; they did, but they went far beyond the Qur'ān, and thus this body of scripture provided also an excellent smoke-screen for doctrines which were entirely un-Qur'ānic.

The corpus of the *Rasā'il* is saturated with the Qur'ān like a sponge and innumerable quotations bear witness to the Ikhwān's deep familiarity with the basic scriptural text of orthodox Islam. In it the Ikhwān are able to find the source, or at least the justification, for many of their ideas.[7] De Boer provides a key to the Ikhwān's sometimes ulterior motives when he rightly points out that the Debate of the Animals allowed the Ikhwān to use the animals as mouthpieces for what might be questionable if spoken by a human.[8] It is striking that the Ikhwān should advise their brethren to read the Christian Gospel and then follow this unorthodox injunction with a long series of Qur'ānic quotations, as if to cloak, or at least minimise, the full impact of their suggestion.[9]

When the Ikhwān quote from the Qur'ān they do not usually name the *sūra* from which each quotation is taken except, unusually, in three places where strings of verses and accompanying *sūra* references are cited.[10] A further exception is *Sūra* 7, *al-A'rāf*, a title which is usually translated as *The Heights* or *The Battlements*, indicating an intermediate place between Paradise and Hell.[11] This *Sūra* does stand out from all the others because of the number of references to it, and to the people who inhabit these Heights, in the *Rasā'il*;[12] this seems to indicate that the *Sūra* was held in special affection by the Ikhwān. It describes, among other things, the missions of the prophets Noah, Hūd, Ṣāliḥ, Lot and Shu'ayb, as well as the conflict between Moses and Pharaoh; and in view of the Ikhwān's concept of the prophets as doctors sent to heal the souls of men it would thus have had a particular significance for them.

Quotations are occasionally commented upon, or briefly explained, by the Ikhwān but there are few attempts at lengthy exegesis (*tafsīr*) of the Qur'ān in any part of the *Rasā'il*. (An exception will be noted a little further on.) The Brethren prefer usually to cite verses in support of a doctrine or view and allow these to speak for themselves. This is not to say that they were unaware of the controversies in Qur'ānic exegesis which flourished through much of the medieval Islamic period. They believed, for example, that Qur'ānic phrases such as *thumma 'stawā 'alā 'l-'arsh*,[13] which A. J. Arberry translates as 'then [He] sat Himself upon the Throne' or 'then seated Himself upon the Throne', had been mistakenly interpreted in an anthropomorphic fashion to indicate a physical 'sitting' (*julūs*) by God. Similarly, the Ikhwān protested against attributes such as seeing and speech being applied to God in their literal human sense. For them, only God and the experts in Qur'ānic exegesis could interpret properly such phrases and verses and explain how they should be applied to God.[14] The Ikhwān believed that the Qur'ān had such experts in mind in the verse 'and whoso is given the Wisdom, has been given much good'[15] and they would certainly have ranked themselves among them. It was thus the wise philosopher who was *uniquely* qualified to undertake the difficult task of interpreting the controversial passages in the Qur'ān; this was a view with which the Spanish Muslim philosopher Ibn Rushd (1126–98) would certainly have sympathised. In their dislike of anthropomorphism, the Ikhwān were closer to the Mu'tazilites, with their penchant for allegorical interpretation, than the rigid Ḥanbalī School with its dogmatic insistence on literalism. As we shall see, however, the Ikhwān's concepts of exegesis of both Qur'ān and Islamic tradition were also tinged with the esotericism of the Ismā'īlīs.

Sometimes, of course, they felt that no comment was necessary or suitable. This was the case, for example, with the isolated groups of Arabic letters which appear occasionally in the Qur'ān, such as the group *Kāf*, *Hā'*, *Yā'*, *'Ayn* and *Ṣād* at the beginning of *Sūra* 19, *The Sūra of Mary*. Although an attempt is made to invest the actual number of such letters with some significance, the Ikhwān conclude that they are really a secret of the Qur'ān and that knowledge about them should remain the province of a few select servants of God.[16]

In one of the rare longer pieces of Qur'ānic exegesis in the *Rasā'il* the Ikhwān discuss the verse 'He sends down out of Heaven water, and the wadis flow each in its measure, and the torrent carries a swelling scum; and out of that over which they kindle fire . . . So God strikes both the true and the false. As for the scum, it vanishes as jetsam, and what profits men abides in the earth.'[17] This verse is invoked by the Ikhwān as a simile for the prophet-legislators responsible for the establishment of the divine law on earth (*wāḍi'ū 'l-nāmūs*), and interpreted as follows: the water sent down from Heaven is the Qur'ān, and the wadis flowing each 'in its measure' indicate the human hearts which commit the Qur'ānic message to memory according to their individual capacities. The scum borne by the torrent is a reference to the sense conveyed by the words of the Qur'ān, a work which contains, on the face of it (*ẓāhiruhu*), a number of obscurities (*mutashābihāt*). But just as the scum in the verse vanishes like jetsam, so profitless falsehoods and obscurities disappear. The concluding words, 'and what profits men abides in the earth', mean that the words of the revelation (*al-tanzīl*) become fixed in the hearts of all true believers and the wisdom (*al-ḥikma*) – that favourite word of the Ikhwān – bears fruit in the minds of men like a good, firmly rooted tree whose branches reach up high into the heavens.[18] This exegesis certainly differs from that of more orthodox interpreters of the Qur'ān such as al-Bayḍāwī (d. 1286 or later).[19]

The desire sometimes to go beyond a superficial or literal (*ẓāhir*) interpretation of a Qur'ānic verse is well demonstrated during the great Debate of the Animals: the king asks for an interpretation of the verse 'We indeed created Man in the fairest stature'.[20] He is told that the prophetic books can be explained other than literally and thus the wise man of the jinn firstly interprets the verse as follows: 'On the day when God created Adam the stars were at their most powerful points (*fī ashrāfihā*),[21] the pivots of the zodiac (*awtād al-burūj*)[22] were upright, and the time was auspicious with a quantity of matter ready to accept form. So man was endowed with the fairest and most perfect of physiques.' The source of the first part of this highly unorthodox piece of astrological *tafsīr*, which gives the position of the stars, has been traced by Yves Marquet to the Hermetic *Kitāb al-Usṭūṭās*.[23]

Despite this, the *Rasā'il* may be said to 'operate' basically from a framework of Qur'ānic orthodoxy. Each epistle, of course, begins with the traditional invocation 'In the Name of God, the Merciful, the Compassionate' (except numbers 1 and 13 in the first section on Mathematical Sciences), but nearly every one is also prefaced, more unusually, with the verse ' "Praise belongs to God, and peace be on His servants whom He has chosen." What, is God better, or that they associate?'[24] The exceptions to this prefatory practice are the early epistles numbered 4, 5, 10, 11, 12, 13 and 14, again in the first section. The verse may be intentionally omitted in the latter five since they all deal with works by Aristotle and Porphyry. Its frequent repetition throughout the *Rasā'il*, however, underlines the emphasis laid by the Ikhwān on the unity of God, but it may also serve as a useful cloak for more unorthodox doctrine such as the concept of emanation. The themes of resignation and submission, implicit in the very word *Islām*, are also emphasised by the frequent quotation of the words 'That is the ordaining of the All-mighty, the All-knowing',[25] which are cited after such natural and astrological phenomena as the formation of rain and the return of the sun after winter to the sign of Aries.[26] The latter is a splendid image for the emergence of the Ikhwān from their cave of concealment and thus the Qur'ānic phrase may be said to underscore *this* emergence as well.

The Qur'ān is used throughout the *Rasā'il* to document particular doctrines and concepts and there is certainly nothing unusual about this: numerous Arab authors have done likewise. Where perhaps the Ikhwān *do* differ is in their similar usage of the Gospel and Torah. The almost mandatory nature of the *Qur'ānic* documentation is acknowledged at the Debate of the Animals where the mule stubbornly maintains that there is no Qur'ānic evidence for human domination over the animals. This is in response to a speech by a human delegate who cites a number of Qur'ānic verses in support of the opposite view.[27]

The characterisation and description of each of the major prophets in the *Rasā'il* are infused with the Qur'ān, though not exclusively influenced by this work. However, A. Guillaume has pointed out that there is a considerable difference between the ways the Qur'ān and the Old Testament treat their characters:

> The stories of the patriarchs and prophets in their original setting are straightforward narratives, which, even if composite in origin, carry the reader forward from the birth to the death of the hero, and present a consecutive, or fairly consecutive, series of events. Not so the Kuran. There the characters are introduced to serve their turn as successful preachers in antiquity of the doctrines promulgated by Muhammad in the present.[28]

The same kind of thing is true of the *Rasā'il*. As we have seen,

philosophers and prophets of Greek, Jewish, Christian and Muslim origin are introduced as evidence of the antiquity of many of the beliefs held by the Ikhwān, such as the immortality of the soul. Since their description of many of these prophets finds its origins in the Qur'ān, it is not surprising that such figures should serve a mainly didactic or illustrative function in the *Rasā'il*. What follows is a short survey of the Qur'ānic substrate on which the portraits of the major prophets in the *Rasā'il* rest, as well as an attempt at identifying some of the instances where non-Qur'ānic material has infiltrated the description.

Adam

References to the traditional Qur'ānic story of Adam and Iblīs, and the latter's pride[29] which prevented him from bowing down to Adam as God commanded after Adam's creation, abound in the *Rasā'il*, particularly in the fourth section.[30] Despite his faults, the Ikhwān are obviously fond of Adam, who is the Islamic prototype of prophethood. They frequently call him 'the Father of Mankind (*Abū 'l-Bashar*)'[31] and acknowledge that he was the first caliph or viceroy (*khalīfa*) to be appointed by God on earth.[32] The first title, 'Father of Mankind', is non-Qur'ānic but the second derives from God's speech to the angels in *Sūra* 2: 'I am setting in the earth a viceroy (*khalīfa*).'[33]

We have already encountered one humoral, non-Qur'ānic description of the creation of Adam in the previous chapter. Elsewhere there is some Judaeo-Christian description mixed in with the Qur'ānic substrate. Adam is created, Qur'ānically, from earth (*turāb*)[34] but he is also created in God's own image and likeness 'according to some of the revealed books', a clear reference to Genesis.[35] The long hair with which the Ikhwān endow the heads of Adam and Eve is not, however, mentioned in the latter, nor in the Qur'ān,[36] but both works do tend to support the idea, so fiercely contested at the Debate of the Animals, that man has dominion over the animals, despite the arguments of the mule which we mentioned earlier.[37] Adam names the trees and the animals in Paradise and this is echoed in the Qur'ān and the Book of Genesis.[38] The Garden of Paradise itself is situated, un-Qur'ānically, by the Ikhwān on the Mount of the Ruby (*Jabal al-Yāqūt*), in the east below the equator.[39]

However, the idyllic life of Paradise, free from tiredness and care and the need to plough and sow to earn a living, is brought to an abrupt end by the Fall. 'Azāzīl tempts Adam and Eve to eat of the forbidden tree. Their eyes are opened and they perceive their nakedness. They are cast out of Paradise onto the inhospitable earth, where they remain lamenting their lot until God takes pity on them and sends an angel – Gabriel in the Islamic tradition – to teach them to plough, sow and cook and generally take care of themselves.[40] The name of Adam became a Qur'ānic prototype of human rebellion against God and as such it is used in the story in the *Rasā'il* of the blind man and the cripple who are compared to Adam and Eve when they are thrown out of the garden from which they steal fruit.[41]

Noah

Noah is one of the prophet-warners who appear in that favourite Qur'ānic *Sūra* of the Ikhwān's, *Sūra* 7, and he also ranks beside Abraham, Moses, Jesus, and Muḥammad as one of 'the Messengers possessed of constancy'.[42] He and his people are saved by God in the ark but Noah's son is drowned after trying in vain to save himself on a mountain.[43] The *Rasā'il* refer to the great flood several times by the Qur'ānic name *al-ṭūfān*[44] and the word is also used metaphorically: the brother who reads the *Rasā'il* is asked whether he would like 'to embark and ride with us in the ship of salvation (*safīnat al-najāt*) which our father Noah built, peace be upon him, so as to be saved from the flood of nature (*ṭūfān al-ṭabī'a*) before 'heaven shall bring a manifest smoke (*bi-dukhān mubīn*)" '.[45] This is a singularly striking and evocative metaphor, providing a good indication of just how rich in overtone, yet compact in style, some of the writing of the Ikhwān can be, often uniting themes and phrases from other parts of the *Rasā'il*: when speaking of Noah the Ikhwān use the word 'ship' (*safīna*) and, indeed, the same metaphor elsewhere,[46] while in another place a Noachic-type flood of water (*ṭūfān min al-mā'*) is envisaged beside a flood of fire (*ṭūfān min al-nār*) like that which the Ikhwān see promised for the end of time in the Qur'ānic words 'when heaven shall bring a manifest smoke'.[47]

Abraham

The portrait of Abraham in the *Rasā'il* is drawn from Judaic as well as Qur'ānic sources. Some of the former, concerning Abraham and Nimrod, have been examined in the last chapter. With regard to the latter, the patriarch is frequently called 'the friend of the Merciful One (*khalīl al-Raḥmān*)',[48] a designation which originates in the Qur'ānic statement that 'God took Abraham for a friend (*khalīl*)'.[49] The Ikhwān claim that their way of thought and kind of life is 'the creed (*milla*) of our father Abraham',[50] thus buttressing the impression of orthodoxy which they are eager to maintain. Indeed, Qur'ānic phrases like 'the creed of your father Abraham' and the more frequent 'the creed of Abraham'[51] constitute a recurring motif which appears in various forms throughout the *Rasā'il*.[52] These epistles, like the Qur'ān, hold that Abraham was the builder of the *Ka'ba* in Mecca[53] and rank him with such famous builders as Solomon, who was responsible for the great Temple in Jerusalem.

The projected sacrifice of Ismā'īl, who replaces the Old Testament Isaac in many Islamic versions of the story, is invoked by the Ikhwān to make a point about the truth and reliability of dreams. Abraham knew that dreams must contain some truth or he would not have resolved to sacrifice his son, and Ismā'īl would not have submitted to such a sacrifice.[54] Ismā'īl is saved at the last moment, ransomed 'with a mighty sacrifice'.[55] The *sūra* does not specify the nature of this sacrifice but the Ikhwān have no doubts: it was a ram which had grazed on the earth of Paradise for forty years.[56] Thus God in His mercy spares the living. Of course, in His power, He can also raise the dead and this is well illustrated by the curious Qur'ānic episode, also cited in the *Rasā'il*, in which four dead birds are revived by God to show Abraham that He is capable of bringing the dead to life.[57]

Joseph

Joseph is designated, Qur'ānically, as 'the true man (*al-ṣiddīq*)',[58] a title which was also borne by the first successor of Muḥammad, Abū Bakr. In Joseph, as in David, Solomon and Muḥammad, are united the qualities of prophethood and kingship.[59] Flung into a well by his brothers,[60] he is taken to Egypt by a passing caravan. His brothers return to their father with a bloodstained shirt and claim that a wolf has devoured Joseph.[61] Joseph rises to a position of fame and power and eventually, after inviting his father and mother to Egypt where he greets them, Joseph eulogises God, saying: 'O my Lord, Thou hast given me to rule, and Thou hast taught me the interpretation of tales. O Thou, the Originator of the heavens and earth, Thou art my Protector in this world and the next. O receive me to Thee in true submission, and join me with the righteous.'[62] The Ikhwān interpret the phrase 'O receive me to Thee in true submission' as a desire for death which is accounted both 'a wisdom and a blessing (*ḥikma wa ni'ma*)', for it finally unites the good soul with all the righteous men who have already passed to eternal life.[63] All this is, of course, very much in keeping with the Ikhwān's basic Platonic idea that the body is a prison for the soul.

Moses and Aaron

Like other major prophets revered by Islam, the figure of Moses occupies a prominent place in the *Rasā'il*; he is recognised as one who speaks with God (*al-kalīm*)[64] and, indeed, converses secretly with Him as a close friend (*najī*).[65] Both epithets are based upon verses in the Qur'ān.[66] His birth is foretold by astrologers and it is stressed that all would have been well for Pharaoh, and indeed Nimrod before him, if the ruler had turned to God, rather than taking the Draconian measures which he did.[67] This is certainly un-Qur'ānic but most of the rest of the story of Moses and Aaron is presented traditionally, with much Qur'ānic quotation throughout the *Rasā'il*. The encounter of Moses and Aaron with Pharaoh is a recurring theme and a graphic illustration of the power of good over evil; this is vividly epitomised in the conversion of Pharaoh's magicians to the faith of Moses and their acceptance of certain death by crucifixion.[68] Moses' story is also briefly summarised by the Jew at the Debate of the Animals: he tells how God parted the sea, drowned Pharaoh and sent down manna and quails to the hungry Israelites.[69] In Moses' absence on Mount Sinai some of his people fall into idolatry and worship a golden calf. When Moses returns, he advises the people how to act in order to win God's pardon and orders the true believers to execute the worshippers of the calf with swords.[70]

The account of the death of Aaron does not occur in the Qur'ān but appears in Islamic legend in a whole variety of forms.[71] In the Ikhwān's version Aaron asks to be allowed to accompany Moses up the mountain, after those who worshipped the calf have been killed. They meet two men digging a grave and are told that the grave is for the man most resembling Aaron. Aaron is asked to test the grave's width and, removing his clothes, he descends into the grave and the Angel of Death seizes his soul. Moses returns, weeping, to the Israelites with the dead man's clothes and is suspected of Aaron's murder but God clears his name.[72] The full significance of Aaron's removal of his clothes, prior to stepping into the grave, is not brought out in this account but other versions show that Aaron was safe from the power of the Angel of Death while he wore his priestly garb.[73] We may compare the story of Aaron in the *Rasā'il* with that, for example, given by al-Ya'qūbī. The latter relates how Moses was inspired by God to take Aaron up the mountain, where they find a couch (*sarīr*) with robes on it. Aaron puts on the robes, stretches out on the couch and dies. God later shows the dead Aaron on the couch to the people of Israel so that they know he is really dead, and Moses is cleared of suspicion.[74] Here the emphasis is clearly on the putting on of pure new garments prior to death, rather than the removal of prophylactic priestly ones, but the substance of the story, which revolves round the dramatic death of Aaron, remains the same. It may be added that much cross-fertilisation obviously took place between the later Haggadic and Islamic versions of the story and these are sometimes difficult to disentangle.[75]

For the Ikhwān, Moses is a law lord (*ṣāḥib sharī'a*) with authority to compel obedience. They contrast him with a strange, Qur'ānic figure, whom they and most exegetes identify as al-Khidr, who was encountered by Moses and his servant at the climax of their journey to 'the meeting of the two seas'. This al-Khidr controls the world of secrets and concealment. There is thus a contrast here between the openness of the divine law (*al-sharī'a*), plainly revealed through such prophets as Moses, and the more shadowy, subterranean world of esoteric interpretation and initially inexplicable action, epitomised in the ambiguous figure of al-Khidr.[76] After the death of Aaron, Moses lingers for a few years, engaged, as a lawgiver, in one final task for the wayward children of Israel, the writing of the Torah. Then he too ascends the mountain to die and the Israelites remain for forty years after his death wandering from the right path.[77]

David

If we compare David with Adam, Abraham or Moses, we find that he appears infrequently in the *Rasā'il*. Nonetheless, like Adam, he receives the solemn title of God's caliph or viceroy (*khalīfa*),[78] which is clearly based on the Qur'ānic verse 'David, behold, We have appointed thee a viceroy (*khalīfa*) in the earth.'[79] He is also described Qur'ānically as 'a penitent (*awwāb*)' as well as one who is 'clement (*ḥalīm*)', an epithet used mostly in the Qur'ān of

God.[80] In David, as in Joseph, Solomon and Muḥammad, the qualities of prophethood and kingship are united.[81] Nonetheless, God's angels have qualities which may surpass even those of the prophets: in a charming sentence we are told that the tunes of the angels as they praise God are better than David's reading of the psalms.[82] The portrait of David is not wholly Qur'ānic: the reference to David's sending Uriah to the front line of battle so that he will be killed, and David's consequent marriage to Uriah's wife, originates in 2 Samuel and not the scripture of Islam.[83] The Qur'ān does, however, portray David as feeling in need of some forgiveness and this may derive from the affair of Uriah.[84]

Solomon

Solomon is revered as the builder of the great Temple of Jerusalem[85] and he is also endowed with a remarkable empathy with the animal world. Not only can he translate the scientific and wisdom literature of the races he conquers into Hebrew[86] but he can also speak the language of the ants and the birds.[87] Indeed, it is the hoopoe, 'friend of the prophet Solomon',[88] who informs him about the Queen of Saba' (Sheba), known to the Arabs as Bilqīs.[89] Solomon has power over the jinn, as well as the devils, mankind, and the animal world.[90] These jinn are forcibly employed in the building of the Temple of Jerusalem, and continue in their task even after the death of Solomon. This is because Solomon dies while resting on his staff and his death goes unsuspected for a whole year until a worm eats through the staff; the staff breaks and Solomon's corpse falls to the ground.[91] The Ikhwān also respect Solomon as a magician: he teaches his soldiers how to catch the jinn with spells and produces a book of magic which is found after his death.[92]

There can be no doubt about the important role which the major Islamic prophets played in the thought of the Ikhwān. Their names permeate the whole text of the *Rasā'il* and the portrayal of each, as we have seen, is always at least partly Qur'ānic. In the four-tier hierarchy of the Brethren, prophets like Abraham, Joseph, Jesus and Muḥammad occupy the angelic rank beside philosophers like Pythagoras and Socrates.[93] This is significant for it indicates that revelation and reason are to be treated equally. It heralds an identification of wisdom (*ḥikma*) and philosophy (*falsafa*), of Islamic *ḥakīm* and Greek philosopher.[94] Thus the wisdom of the Qur'ān itself is no longer to be viewed as something completely isolated from Neoplatonism but as a complementary and fertile source of inspiration and backing for the Ikhwān's corpus of doctrine in which both Qur'ānic revelation and pagan dogma and philosophy have a place. The Islamic orthodoxy of the former may, at the same time, attempt to cloak the wilder Neoplatonic heresies of the latter from hostile eyes.

INDIAN LITERATURE

The *Rasā'il* contain not only Greek, Judaeo-Christian, and Qur'ānic influences but also a variety of Persian, Indian, Buddhist, Zoroastrian, and Manichaean elements as well. The culture of the Eastern Islamic world was clearly as familiar to their authors as that of the Western, and in view of the cosmopolitan nature of the city of Baṣra, where they are traditionally thought to have lived,[95] this is not surprising. This familiarity is demonstrated in a small way by the Persian vocabulary[96] and quotations of inferior Persian verse which occur in the text[97] as well as by the citation of names of Persian kings such as Ardashīr I (*reg.* AD 226–41), from whose Testament (*Waṣiyya*) they quote.[98]

It is demonstrated much more obviously in some of their stories and anecdotes. Two kinds predominate in the *Rasā'il* and they may be labelled respectively 'King Stories' and 'Animal Stories'. The former clearly owed much to the East: Persia, for example, had a literature which abounded in epics about kings. The number of 'King Stories' which appear in the *Rasā'il* attests to the popularity which this kind of story had gained in the milieu of the Ikhwān by the time at which they wrote. These stories obviously belong to a recognised and clearly defined genre for they have several stylistic features in common: they often begin with phrases like 'They related that one of the kings of India . . .' and go on to describe the might and sovereignty of a king who is considered to be a good or wise ruler to his subjects.[99]

Perhaps the most famous and important of the 'King Stories' in the *Rasā'il* are those taken from the legend of Bilawhar and Yūdāsaf (or Būdhāsaf), who were known in medieval Europe as Barlaam and Josaphat or Joasaph. S. M. Stern believed that the *Rasā'il* were 'perhaps the earliest testimony for the existence of this Indian legend in an Arabic translation',[100] and several Arabic versions are known to have existed. The legend, whose origins lie in the story of the Buddha, was translated from Pahlavi into Arabic by Ibn al-Muqaffa' (died *c.* 756) and his school, and also incorporated in a Shī'ite work by Ibn Bābūya (or Ibn Bābawayhi, d. 991). It is the tale of a prince named Yūdāsaf who is brought up in total ignorance of human distress by being kept within the confines of a city. Tiring of this at last, he rides out and encounters human infirmity and old age for the first time. He also meets a hermit from Ceylon called Bilawhar who persuades him to adopt the life of an ascetic. Yūdāsaf converts his father, undertakes a number of adventurous missionary journeys and eventually dies in Kashmir.[101]

The Ikhwān were clearly aware of the Indian origins of the legend since, in the speech of the Indian during the Debate of the Animals, Būdāsaf [*sic*] and Bilawhar are included, with the Buddha and the Brahmans, in a list of prophets and wise men of India.[102] The former prince and the hermit were highly esteemed by the Brethren, who placed them in the fourth and highest rank of their hierarchy, in the company of such distinguished prophets and sages as Abraham, Joseph, Christ, Muḥammad, Socrates and Pythagoras, and did not hesitate to quote from them concerning the importance of knowledge about the Kingdom of Heaven.[103]

Yet the Ikhwān often omitted to link the stories which they drew from the Bilawhar legend with the legend by name. This is certainly the case in the story of the poor but happy couple encountered by a king and his wazīr, which also constitutes an interesting example in the epistles of 'framework technique', in which one story is told within another.[104] The narrator is referred to only as 'the wise man (*al-ḥakīm*)' and, earlier, as 'one of the wise men of Ceylon'.[105] The story itself tells how a king goes for a walk one night with his wazīr and they see a light in the distance. They meet a man and a woman living in a large dunghill who are entirely happy with their poverty-stricken state, drinking, dancing and singing together and endowing each other with grand titles. The king is amazed at their happiness and the wazīr seizes the opportunity to preach the merits of piety, asceticism and the joys of the Kingdom of God to his king.[106]

Another tale taken from the Bilawhar legend and transmitted in the *Rasā'il* is that of the prince who sleeps with a corpse. Again the framework technique is used. A king marries his son to another king's daughter and one night, during the celebrations, the son walks out of the city into the desert, rather drunk, and loses himself. Seeing a light in the distance he goes towards it and finds a group of people asleep. Thinking that he has returned to the bride's chamber and that the sleepers are her servants, he lies down beside the woman he thinks is his bride and embraces her. In the sober light of morning he wakes to find that all the people are, in fact, dead, and that he has slept with a corpse. He obtains some fresh clothes from a passer-by after washing in a river and is able to return to his former happiness.[107]

The didactic nature of the parable is clear, and the wise man, and through him the Ikhwān, uses it to stress the idea that the soul, once separated from the body and risen to Heaven, certainly does not long to return to that body, any more than the prince longs to return to the corpse with which he has spent the night. There is thus an intriguing mixture of Platonic philosophy and Buddhistic legend here in the *Rasā'il* which is further evidence of the continuity of the Ikhwān's syncretic approach throughout their writings. Furthermore, we may note in passing that it is only after self-purification in a river that the prince returns to his former state; this reiterates a major theme of the epistles.

Elsewhere, the Ikhwān use another story from the Bilawhar corpus – the story of the gem – to make the point that their Brethren should choose wise young men to whom to impart their wisdom and knowledge. A son is born to a good but idol-worshipping king of India. The son grows up to be very learned and his thoughtful nature makes him yearn to consult a wise man about the things which perplex him. The wise Ceylonese, whom we mentioned above, hears about him and travels to see him. He asks a servant of the king's son to tell the son that he has brought him a gift of precious jewels. By this ruse he gains admission to the presence of the prince and the latter is able to question him about all the matters which trouble and vex him.[108]

The theme of the philosopher or prophet as the doctor of souls is a common one in the *Rasā'il*. In one place the prophets are likened to a doctor who visits a town where all the inhabitants are ill without knowing it. By exercising great patience, the doctor succeeds in curing them one by one. Once again we find that this is another story in the *Rasā'il* which has its origins in the Bilawhar legend, and once again it is one which the Ikhwān have adopted for their own didactic purposes.[109]

Considerable emphasis has been placed upon the appearance of the legend of Bilawhar in the *Rasā'il* because the extent to which the Ikhwān drew upon it, for didactic material with which to preach their theme of immortality won by the ascetic life, has not been sufficiently stressed nor appreciated. D. M. Lang, for example, refers only to 'the allusion in the *Rasā'il*' to the fable of the Happy Poor Couple.[110] However, such lack of emphasis may be due to the fact that the main stories in the *Rasā'il* taken from the Bilawhar legend are often not directly associated with that legend by name.

If we turn to the second category of stories in which the Ikhwān specialise, the 'Animal Story', we find that here too the influences are from India and the East. The fullest example of the 'Animal Story' in the *Rasā'il* is the great Debate of the Animals which occupies a considerable portion of the *Risāla* entitled *On How the Animals and their Kinds are Formed*.[111] At this Debate representatives of the animal and human worlds appear before a *Shāh* to debate the question of whether man is superior to the animals. Man, it seems, has pressed into his service such animals as cattle, sheep, camels and horses, filled with a boundless conviction that he is superior to them and that they have been created to serve him. But he has severely maltreated them while making them serve. So the animals go to the *Shāh* of the jinn and complain to him about man's injustice towards them. A debate is convened. Delegates from both mankind and the animal kingdom speak at length, often larding their addresses to the assembled multitude with a mass of Qur'ānic quotation designed to underline the points which the speaker is making. Finally, following a speech by the Ikhwān's ideal man,[112] judgement is given by the *Shāh* in favour of man, at least for the time being.[113]

The question of whether man was, in fact, superior to the animals, had obviously aroused some debate in Baṣra. The Baṣran al-Jāḥiẓ, for example, also considered the question in his *Book of the Animals* (*Kitāb al-Ḥayawān*) and concluded, in one place at least, that man *was* superior to all the other denizens of the animal kingdom. The real difference for al-Jāḥiẓ between man and the animals lay in man's capability or capacity (*istiṭā'a*), a concept which presupposed the existence of both reason and cognition.[114]

The profoundly anthropomorphic nature of this Debate of the Animals, where the animals are endowed with such faculties as speech and thought, owes much to antecedents such as *Kalīla wa Dimna*, the collection of Indian fables which was rendered into

Arabic from Pahlavi by Ibn al-Muqaffaʿ, but whose ultimate origins lie in the Sanskrit *Panchatantra*.[115] The names of both Kalīla and Dimna, in fact, reappear in the *Rasāʾil* during the Debate: we find that the beasts of prey are represented by the same jackal, 'Kalīla, brother of Dimna', who is described by the tiger as being 'wise, just, knowledgeable and experienced'.[116] Kalīla's role here, of course, is very small by comparison with that which he plays in Ibn al-Muqaffaʿ 's work, but it is nonetheless significant since it signals a desire by the Ikhwān that their own Debate should have some link with the great *Kalīla wa Dimna*.

There are several other links as well between the Ikhwān's writings and this work of Ibn al-Muqaffaʿ. These include the story of the ring-dove and that of the owls and the crows. The significance of the first in the history of the *Rasāʾil* has been examined in the first chapter and will not be pursued here.[117] The story of the owls and the crows is interesting since it is cited by the Ikhwān as a simile of the man who defends himself by trickery: the crows, who have been much harassed by an army of owls, send a fifth columnist into the owls' camp; as a result, the crows are eventually able to burn the owls' dwellings and destroy their enemies.[118] One of the stories told within the framework of this main story in both *Kalīla wa Dimna* and the *Panchatantra* is invoked in another part of the *Rasāʾil* to illustrate the saying that 'many a word has brought about discord and wars'. The Ikhwān allege that the enmity between the owls and the crows resulted from a word which the crow spoke when the birds met to make the owl king; for the crow successfully persuaded the birds against the owl's election by telling a number of fables.[119]

Two of the animal fables in the *Rasāʾil* are clearly labelled as Indian in origin by the Ikhwān. The first concerns a group of foxes who go out in search of something to eat. They find a dead camel which they decide to share. A passing wolf is persuaded to divide the camel between them. He does so but later considers his kindly act to be weakness and desires the food for himself. When the foxes come to him in the morning to receive more of the carcass, the wolf makes one more division of meat and warns the foxes not to return for any more since he will keep the rest for himself. The hungry foxes hope that once the wolf has eaten his fill he will relent and divide the rest among them. They go to plead with the wolf but he is obdurate. The foxes therefore take themselves to the lion, the king of the beasts of prey, and relate their story to him. The lion seizes the wolf and tears him to pieces; the dead camel is then returned to the foxes. The Ikhwān conclude their tale with a thoroughly Aesopic moral to the effect that one calamity is always capped by another.[120]

The second tale deals with the relationship between some crows and a falcon and is used as a parable for the nation which ignores the advice of its prophet when choosing a new ruler. The crows are blessed with a good king who dies. They disagree over his successor and hold a council to debate the issue where they decide that they do not wish to choose a member of the former king's family. Their misguided choice falls on an undernourished falcon whom they make king. The falcon grows to his former strength and begins to tyrannise and kill the crows. Before his death he appoints an even more vicious successor from his race, and the crows repent too late of their initial choice.[121]

These two tales, which resemble the type which is found in *Kalīla wa Dimna*, follow a similar pattern: they are both taken from 'the fables of India', and they are both cited for didactic illustration by the Ikhwān. Indeed, there is little if any narrative in the *Rasā'il* which is designed for the pure entertainment of the reader and no other purpose.

The sheer diversity of the milieu in which the Ikhwān must have lived is never more clearly demonstrated than in such scattered elements of Indian and Persian literature, culture, religion, language and thought as appear in the *Rasā'il*. Furthermore, the inclusion of references to writings attributed to Ibn al-Muqaffa', who spent much of his life in Baṣra, and who was suspected of being a Manichee, has not been sufficiently emphasised in previous studies. It is true that there are many more Greek and Christian elements in the *Rasā'il* than, for example, Indian, Zoroastrian or Manichaean; but when the latter are added to all the other non-Islamic elements in these epistles the final picture which emerges is of a group of philosophers constantly searching for fresh parallels with which to illustrate, prove, sustain and propagate their own doctrine, with the inevitable influences which such a cross-cultural search must produce. Indeed, the purity which the Ikhwān sought was often very similar to that for which both Plato and Mani strove.

CHAPTER SIX

The Ikhwān al-Ṣafā' and the Ismā'īlīs

In the first chapter attention was drawn to the difficulties involved in fixing an exact date of composition for the *Rasā'il*.[1] Yet an exact dating is by no means necessary to show that the Ikhwān lived in an age of widespread sectarianism. Their *Rasā'il* manifest a keen awareness of the divisive climate in which they lived: 'Know that people differ in their doctrines (*ārā'*) and religious creeds (*madhāhib*) just as they differ in the forms of their bodies.'[2] Not only do they twice give lists of different sects of the prevailing Middle Eastern religions,[3] (for 'you also find people of one religion having different religious creeds and doctrines'[4]), but they devote a whole chapter to the study of doctrines and religions.[5] In this they recognise that differences in knowledge and intellectual ability can be prime factors in the acceptance or rejection of particular doctrines and creeds,[6] and they go on to cite a variety of other causes of sectarianism. These include different levels of imagination,[7] bad use of analogical reasoning (*qiyās*),[8] and seeking to solve the problem of evil in the world[9] as well as such contentious questions as those of the Imāmate,[10] the attributes of God,[11] and free will.[12] Textual problems and the exegesis of passages which could bear more than one meaning were a further fertile source of sectarian dispute.[13]

Yet the Ikhwān believed that considerable good could also come from religious differences, since they would provoke souls to seek knowledge and truth and wake from the sleep of ignorance. In a restrained and unpartisan fashion they described the differences among the scholars in their doctrines and religious creeds as 'a mercy (*ikhtilāf al-'ulamā' raḥma*)', and the differences of the religionists (*ahl al-diyānāt*) in religion and its normative provisions as 'a wisdom (*ḥikma*)'.[14] These descriptions are immediately evocative of the saw of medieval Islamic law that difference in the community was a sign of the divine bounty or mercy.

Strangely enough, in their two lists of sects and their chapter on doctrines and religions, the Ikhwān do not mention the Ismā'īlīs though many other diverse sects such as the Qadariyya[15] and the Sabaeans of Ḥarrān[16] do appear. Yet it was the Ismā'īlī sect, perhaps more than any other, which had the most profound effect on the structure and vocabulary of the Ikhwān. It is in the Ismā'īlīs that the sectarianism of the age is best epitomised by virtue of the high degree of organisation, hierarchy and elaborate doctrine which that sect developed.[17]

The relationship between the Ismā'īlīs and the Ikhwān al-Ṣafā' has been viewed up to now in a similar light by scholars. Nearly all have attempted to show that the Ikhwān were definitely Ismā'īlīs; the possibility that they may have been merely influenced by Ismā'īlī thought, without actually being Ismā'īlīs, has provoked less consideration. Fyzee observed, for example, that 'the tracts are clearly of Ismā'īlī origin; and all authorities, ancient and modern, are agreed that the *Rasā'il* constitute the most authoritative exposition of the early form of the Ismā'īlī religion'.[18] Yves Marquet considers that 'it seems indisputable that the Epistles represent the state of Ismā'īlī doctrine at the time of their composition'[19] and many other authorities have shared this view. Hossein Nasr observes that 'it is not surprising to find most modern scholars, Muslims and non-Muslims alike, claiming Ismā'īlī authorship for the work'.[20] After a useful review of the work of such scholars, to which the reader is referred,[21] Nasr himself concludes that 'we may loosely connect the Ikhwān with Ismā'īlism, especially with what has been called "Ismā'īlī gnosis" '.[22]

Yet there *have* been a few reservations. S. M. Stern wrote:

> It is obvious that the authors of the Epistles, though they were connected with Ismā'īlism, elaborated a peculiar doctrine which was not at all acceptable to the main body of the movement. Thus, while in the fifth/eleventh century the teaching of the Epistles exercised a considerable influence on philosophic and scientific circles unconnected with Ismā'īlism, there is no trace of the influence of the Epistles among the Ismā'īlī authors of the period.[23]

Stern went on to argue that the Ikhwān were an idealised Ismā'īlī movement out of tune with contemporary mainstream Ismā'īlism.[24] Lewis, too, was more cautious than Fyzee, ranking the *Rasā'il* among books which, though 'closely related to Ismā'īlism', may not actually have been Ismā'īlī,[25] despite their Bāṭinī (that is, Ismā'īlī) inspiration.[26] Tibawi, while noting that 'there is sufficient evidence in the tracts themselves to prove Ismā'īlī sympathies', points out that there is still no proof that the institution of a group called Ikhwān al-Ṣafā', and the resulting publication of their *Rasā'il*, was an Ismā'īlī movement.[27] 'A. 'Awā in his work, too, takes a non-Ismā'īlī view[28] and some of his observations will be referred to later on. Most recently, Hossein Nasr appears to have revised his opinions somewhat for he writes: 'This group of authors, whose identity has never become completely clear, was certainly of Shī'ī inspiration although perhaps not as specifically Ismā'īlī as it came to be considered later.'[29] The Italian scholar Alessandro Bausani emphasises this with his succinct question and answer: 'Are the *Ikhwān al-Ṣafā'* Ismā'īlīs? The point has not yet been decided with certainty. . . .'[30]

In his article referred to above, Fyzee rightly points out that 'Ismā'īlism was a sect of the Shī'ites which developed an extreme doctrine of the Imamate; it placed 'Ali far above the Prophet'.[31] But there is a contradiction between his description of the Ikhwān as Ismā'īlīs and this later statement which will become apparent in the following pages.

The argument which the question of the Imāmate inspired in Islam was continuous and fierce. The heresiographer al-Shahrastānī (1086–1153) was moved to observe that it was this question which had caused the greatest dissension in the whole Islamic community and that no doctrine had provoked such bloodshed in Islam in every age as the doctrine of the Imāmate.[32]

The Ismā'īlīs made the Imāmate a cardinal doctrine of faith. Obedience to the *Imāms* was obedience to God and disobedience to them was disobedience to God. Thus the Ismā'īlī *Qāḍī* al-Nu'mān (d. 974) wrote: 'The *Imāms* of right guidance, may they be blessed, are among the creatures and chosen servants of God most glorious. God has enjoined obedience to every *Imām* among them on the people of his age, and imposed on them submission to his authority. He has made the *Imāms* leaders of His creatures to Him and guides of His servants to Him.'[33] He cites a *ḥadīth* from Ja'far al-Ṣādiq concerning the Qur'ānic verse, 'O believers, obey

God, and obey the Messenger and those in authority among you.'[34] The latter are interpreted by Ja'far as 'the *Imāms* among us to whom obedience is enjoined'.[35] This stress on obedience to the *Imāms* is in marked contrast to the casuistry of the Sunnī jurists who sought to reconcile the disobedience of many breakaway rulers from the Caliph with traditional theory.

In common with the Ithnā 'Asharī branch of Shī'ism, the Ismā'īlīs rejected the Sunnī doctrine of election. Since they believed that 'Alī had been directly nominated by Muḥammad, election was wrong. The *Imām* could not be chosen by the people, who would never in any case have agreed on one man because of their differences,[36] but he was given his position by the designation (*naṣṣ*) of his predecessor. Though human, he was considered sinless and infallible and his decisions were absolute and irrevocable. Legally the *Imām* was 'the final interpreter of the law on earth'[37] and his word was ranked by the *Qāḍī* al-Nu'mān beside the Qur'ān and *Sunna* as one of the three foundations of the law.[38]

Ismā'īlī Islam thus held the *Imām* in far greater esteem and awe than Sunnī Islam, where he could be deposed, or forfeit the Imāmate, if necessity or circumstance warranted it.[39] It would therefore be impossible to be an Ismā'īlī and at the same time deny the Imāmate or be in any way hesitant or grudging in its support. Yet the Ikhwān al-Ṣafā, so often described as Ismā'īlīs, were more than lukewarm in their devotion to this doctrine. As will be shown, they replaced the concept of Imāmate with that of brotherhood.

Their whole attitude to the doctrine of the Imāmate is characterised by a considerable vagueness of approach. The clear treatment which Hamdānī claims to find sometimes in the *Rasā'il* is more assumed than real.[40] It is by no means clear that the eschatological titles he cites, such as 'Supreme Master of the Law (*Ṣāḥib al-Nāmūs al-Akbar*)',[41] refer to an *Imām* at all.[42] Even Yves Marquet, in one place, was forced to describe the *Rasā'il* as 'pudiquement voilés' on the question of the Imāmate.[43]

Like al-Shahrastānī, the Ikhwān recognised the troubles and bloodshed to which the doctrine had given rise in Islamic history:

> Know that the question of the Imāmate is also one of the original subjects of dispute among the scholars. Those who have tackled it have become lost in all kinds of arguments and a lot of nonsense has been talked on the subject. Enmity and

> hatred have appeared among its exponents, and warfare and strife have broken out between its students. Expenditure and bloodshed have been justified because of it. The problem has persisted into our own age. Indeed, those who tackle it increase every day and dispute about it with one argument set against another. The subject has given rise to so many doctrines and religious creeds that only God can count their number.[44]

The Ikhwān note that some believed that the Imāmate should be held by designation (*naṣṣ*) by those closest in lineage to the Prophet Muḥammad, while others held the opposite.[45]

Contrary to Hamdānī's assertion, however, and despite the technical terminology which he offers as evidence,[46] the *Imām* is not 'the central point for the mission (*da'wat*) of the Rasā'il'. His role is *directly* spoken of in only a few places.[47] Furthermore, the whole usage by the Ikhwān of the words *khalīfa* (caliph or viceroy) and *Imām* is both loose and eclectic in application: Adam is described Qur'ānically as God's *khalīfa* on earth[48] while in the Debate of the Animals all human kings are called *khulafā'* (caliphs) of God on earth.[49] He who seeks to become the *khalīfa* of God with bad intentions becomes the *khalīfa* of Iblīs.[50] Passion is also described as the *khalīfa* of Iblīs and the brother is urged to make reason (*'aql*) the *khalīfa* over his soul,[51] and to be a guide and a *mahdī*, terms traditionally applied to the *Imām*.[52] The *Imām*s themselves are described as *khulafā'* of the prophets.[53]

Nowhere do the Ikhwān manifest a great enthusiasm specifically for the doctrine of the Imāmate, let alone 'une conviction ardente, parfois fanatique'.[54] On the contrary, they can do without an *Imām*:

> Know that if the minds of good, wise men received additionally the power (*al-quwwa*) possessed by the *wāḍi' al-sharī'a*,[55] they would not need a leader to lead them and command them, forbid them [from evil] and restrain and govern them, because the intellect (*al-'aql*) and the power (*al-qudra*) of the *wāḍi' al-nāmūs* take the place of the leader, the *Imām* (*al-ra'īs al-Imām*). So come with us, O brother, that we may follow the norms (*sunna*) of the holy law (*sharī'a*) and make it an *Imām* for us in what we have resolved upon.[56]

This brief but very important paragraph, the full implications of which most scholars seem to have ignored, not only clearly shows that the office of *Imām* may be dispensed with, but, by its separation of the offices of *wāḍi' al-sharī'a*, *wāḍi' al-nāmūs* and *Imām*, does much to disprove the theory put forward by Marquet that the three terms are synonymous.[57]

Elsewhere the Ikhwān show that though recognition of the *khalīfa* is useful as an aid to salvation it is not obligatory: as noted before, the brother may substitute reason (*'aql*) and be guided by this, accepting its dictates and prohibitions but avoiding passion: 'Then make your reason the *khalīfa* over your soul.'[58]

It is true that the extolling of visits to the mosques and tombs of saints and martyrs,[59] the unequivocally 'Alid language used of the Battle of Ṣiffīn,[60] and the glorification of al-Ḥusayn and the Battle of Karbalā',[61] indicate distinctly Shī'ite sympathies on the part of the Ikhwān. Such sympathy is perhaps neatly summed up in the speech of the Khurāsānī from Merv at the Debate of the Animals: 'We ourselves wore black and sought vengeance for the blood of al-Ḥusayn; we expelled the tyrants of the Banū Marwān.'[62] But the acute hostility which some scholars have seen in their attitude to the Caliphs of the Umayyad and 'Abbāsid dynasties[63] can be exaggerated. 'Alī is indeed respected as the leader of the Islamic community (*Amīr al-Mu'minīn*)[64] but this respect is not mixed with fanaticism.[65] The Caliphs who succeeded him do not provide a *constantly* reiterated focus for Shi'a-inspired hatred throughout the *Rasā'il*, though these epistles do evince *some* distaste for their dynasties.[66]

In a long list of early followers of Muḥammad, Abū Bakr, the successor of the Prophet, who is here described as the Prophet's friend, appears immediately after 'Alī.[67] A few lines further on, 'Umar b. al-Khaṭṭāb, the second Caliph, is spoken of in similarly reverent tones. If the Ikhwān had been fanatical Shī'ites, we would have expected them to exult over the murder of the third Caliph, 'Uthmān b. 'Affān. But the reverse is the case. The Ikhwān observe that one of the qualities of the true believer is contentment with fate and the divine decree.[68] After Socrates and Christ they mention 'Uthmān as an example and admiringly cite his behaviour when confronted by his assassins (in AD 656).[69] The Ikhwān even cite 'Umar's recommendation to read certain *sūra*s of the Qur'ān[70] and he is here given the salutation, applied to friends of the Prophet, 'May God be pleased with him (*raḍiya*

Allāh 'anhu).' All this is in marked contrast to the hatred of the extreme Shī'ites for the early successors of the Prophet.[71]

'A. 'Awā has identified four principal characteristics in the Shī'ite *Imām*: infallibility, return, Messianism and dissimulation of religion in time of danger (*taqiyya*).[72] But the infallibility (*'iṣma*) of the *Imām*, that fundamental of Ismā'īlism, is hardly mentioned in the *Rasā'il*, much less extolled. It is not among the qualities of the *wādi' al-sharī'a*, whom Marquet identifies with both prophet and *Imām*,[73] nor one of his necessary beliefs,[74] nor a requisite of the Imāmate-Caliphate in its prophetic aspect,[75] nor a characteristic of the royal temporal aspect of the Caliphate.[76]

With regard to the linked concepts of return and Messianism, the emphasis throughout the *Rasā'il* is much more on the return of the individual soul to God than the return of the *Imām*, and the body is considered, Platonically, as a prison for the individual soul.[77] The eschatological figure of the expected *Mahdī* (*al-Mahdī al-Muntaẓar*) appears only rarely in the *Rasā'il* and he seems, unexpectedly, to be linked in some way with the Paraclete.[78] Yet surely any text in which the role for the *Imām* was *really* stressed might be expected to give considerable prominence to the sublime figure of the *Mahdī*, who had such an enormous significance in the Shī'ite tradition. Instead we find that the Messianism of the *Rasā'il* is limited to the occasional unelaborated reference such as we have just mentioned, or to stereotyped spokesmen like the Khurāsānī at the Debate of the Animals who proclaims in stridently Shī'ite terms: 'We hope that there will appear from our country the *Imām*, the *Mahdī*, peace be upon him, who is the Expected One (*al-Muntaẓar*) from the House of Muḥammad . . .'.[79]

Reference is certainly made in the *Rasā'il* to concealment of religion though not necessarily under the name *taqiyya*,[80] and there is a reiteration of such words as 'veiling (*satr*)' and 'revelation' or 'disclosure' (*kashf*) especially in the *Jāmi'a*.[81] Discussing their feasts the Ikhwān wrote: 'Then the fourth day is the day of sadness and sorrow, the day of our return to our cave and the cave of *taqiyya* and concealment (*al-istitār*).'[82] But there is no persistently didactic emphasis on a doctrine of *taqiyya* in the *Rasā'il* such as would justify ascribing to the Ikhwān the attitude expressed in the statement attributed to Ja'far al-Ṣādiq: '*Taqiyya* is my religion and the religion of my fathers in everything. . . .'[83] On the contrary, the Ikhwān in one place positively reject the idea of a hidden or concealed *Imām*: 'Among them [the Shī'a] are those who say that the expected *Imām* is hidden (*mukhtafin*) for fear of those who would disagree with him. This is by no means the case for he is manifest (*ẓāhir*) in their midst. . . '.[84] Thus there seems to be little truth in the assertion that the Ikhwan's reiterated command to turn from the sleep of negligence and the slumber of ignorance symbolises the clandestinity of the *Imām*.[85]

The Ikhwān al-Ṣafā', while paying lip-service to the traditional doctrine of the Imāmate by the occasional unenthusiastic reference, replaced the whole concept with that of brotherhood (*ukhuwwa*). The key to this lies in the following statement of theirs:

> Know, O brother, that if these qualities [the forty-six prophetical qualities] are united simultaneously in one human being, during one of the cycles of astral conjunctions, then that person is the Delegate (*al-Mab'ūth*) and the Master of the Age (*Ṣāḥib al-Zamān*) and the *Imām* for the people as long as he lives. If he fulfils his mission (*risāla*) and accomplishes his allotted task, advises the community (*al-umma*) and records the revelation, codifies its [correct] interpretation (*ta'wīl*) and consolidates the holy law (*al-sharī'a*), clarifies its method (*minhāj*) and implements the traditional procedures (*al-sunna*) and welds the community into one; [if he does all that and] then dies and passes away, those qualities will remain in his community as its heritage. If those qualities, or most of them, are united in one man in his community, then he is the man suited to be his successor (*khalīfatahu*) in his community after his death. But if it does not happen that those qualities are united in one man, but are scattered among all its members, and they speak with one voice and their hearts are united in love for each other, and they co-operate in supporting the faith, preserving the law and implementing the *sunna*, and bearing the community along the path of religion, then their dynasty will endure in this world and the outcome will be happy for them in the next. But if that community is disunited after the death of its prophet and disagrees on the path of religion, the unity of their friendship will be dissolved and things will go badly for them in the hereafter and their dynasty will vanish. So if you are determined to seek the betterment of [both your] religion and the world, then come with us! We meet with a group of distin-

guished brothers and follow the *sunna* of the law in sincere behaviour, genuine advice and pure brotherhood (*ṣafwat al-ukhuwwa*).[86]

This important statement clearly shows that the Ikhwān believed that a community could in fact dispense with the *Imām* and still achieve salvation.[87] At first, the *Imām* is placed on a pedestal as the sum total of all the virtues. But by the end there is an acknowledgement that, provided these virtues are present in a unified community (*umma*), the *Imām* is to all intents and purposes superfluous. The purpose of the Ikhwān becomes clear in the last exhortation: the unified community of the Ikhwān is a repository of all the above-mentioned virtues and as such replaces any need for an *Imām*. The equation of *umma* and Ikhwān becomes complete.

The Ikhwān go on to observe that there is no group better able to help in matters of religion or worldly affairs with mutual good advice than the Ikhwān. Each of its members believed that he could only properly exalt the faith by helping his brother, and seeking for him what he sought for himself.[88] The school or way of life of the Ikhwān meant showing mercy and kindness to all;[89] thus the brother with money but no knowledge should help the penniless scholar who in turn should be equally generous with his knowledge.[90] Their friendship did not change, for the Ikhwān considered themselves to be one soul in several bodies.[91] Thus, where the jurist al-Māwardī (d. 1058) laid a heavy burden of ten basic responsibilities on his Sunnī *Imām*,[92] the Ikhwān reduced this to the single, lighter burden of friendship (*ṣadāqa*) imposed on every member of a brotherhood which replaced in action as well as name the traditional doctrine of the Imāmate.

Though the need for a leader (*ra'īs*) in the community is at times also acknowledged, this does not invalidate any of what has been said. For the Ikhwān claimed to be content with their own leader which was the human reason (al-'aql) 'which God most glorious has made leader over the best of His creation', and they observed that they would rigorously avoid the company of anyone who was not content with 'the dictates of reason (*sharā'iṭ al-'aql*)'.[93] As we have seen, it was reason which should have a Caliphal supremacy over man's soul.

In view of the essential nature of the Imāmate to the Ismā'īlīs, and the inferior role allocated to the Imāmate by the Ikhwān, it may be concluded that the Ikhwān were not Ismā'īlīs. The *Rasā'il* should not therefore be described, in the words of one scholar, as the oldest account of Ismā'īlī doctrine.[94] The Ismā'īlī elements found in the *Rasā'il* are reducible to the level of influences and should not be regarded as indigenous factors in the doctrine of the Ikhwān.

CONCLUSION

The Ship of Salvation

The Ikhwān indeed practised a philosophy of tolerance and eclecticism in their *Rasā'il*, but the previous chapters show that such a description should be used with care and applied with several caveats: it was primarily in the field of textual borrowing and reference that the Ikhwān most manifested their penchant for eclecticism. They did not disdain to borrow from the whole spectrum of world scripture, pagan philosophy and Abrahamic theology. The range at their disposal was vast for diversity of thought was the keynote of the Middle Eastern milieu in which they wrote. It was a milieu which had produced works as disparate as those filled with the satirical invective of al-Jāḥiẓ, on the one hand, and those imbued with the Neoplatonism of the author of the *Theologia* and others infected by the spirit of Plotinus, on the other; a milieu in which the Bible had already been translated into a number of vernacular languages and also supplemented by a variety of apocryphal testaments; and a milieu in which Ismā'īlism was expanding rapidly to receive its political apotheosis with the Fāṭimid seizure of Egypt in AD 969.

However, the use of texts of other religions and philosophies by the Ikhwān does not mean that they *uncritically* accepted the dogma of every religion whose texts they used. Though, as we have seen, they were often profoundly influenced by such works, they did not hesitate to criticise where they found it necessary. Thus they castigated the Jews at times but elsewhere accepted the Torah as having an equal value with the Qur'ān and the Gospel as a primary source. They virulently inveighed against the faults of other religions, and indeed, against those of Islam itself,[1] through the mouth of the Strong Man (*Ṣāḥib al-'Azīma*) at the great Debate of the Animals, using him as an orthodox disguise for their own multifarious unorthodoxies.

It was inevitable that the ambivalence of their eclecticism, epitomised in acceptance of the text but not necessarily of all that the text's religion or philosophy taught, should have led to some confusion about their own beliefs. Furthermore, it was impossible, then as now, for any group to maintain an attitude of total tolerance to a variety of mutually hostile and often intolerant religions and creeds without some contradiction creeping in. This is seen most vividly in the Ikhwān's view of God, where they attempted to identify the Neoplatonic One with the Islamic Allāh. Elsewhere, their account of the life of Jesus, and especially the crucifixion, contains, in one place at least, a statement of facts quite at variance with the Qur'ānic account. The necessity of continuing to teach while at the same time avoiding confrontation added a further dimension in which it may sometimes have been necessary to make *deliberately* contradictory statements as a form of *taqiyya*.[2]

With all this in mind, the Ikhwān appear, perhaps, reluctant Muslims. Yet they have been described as truly Islamic because of a belief that what was historically eclectic in the *Rasā'il* was gathered together with one Islamic end in mind, and that their aim was 'to build a unified citadel'.[3] According to this view the multiplicity of the Ikhwān's source material was thus funnelled to a unicity or single purpose which was the Islamic God and the Islamic exaltation of His oneness.[4] This might have been an attractive way of viewing the Ikhwān were it not for the fact that, as has been shown, the Ikhwān's concept of God differed radically from that of orthodox Islam; and, indeed, many of their beliefs were entirely outside the pale of Islam. A better way of considering the Ikhwān's thought might be to see it as a series of lines radiating outwards and touching the circumference of world beliefs rather than as a variety of schools of thought and religious beliefs beamed inwards on the focus of Islam. It is true that the Ikhwān too had a single focus for which they derived inspiration and support from the many beliefs with which they came into contact, but that focus was the universal concept of purity, and not Islam.

A keyword in the methodology of the Ikhwān was adaptation. They frequently adapted what they found in other religions, and philosophies such as Pythagoreanism, to their own ends. One scholar has asked in what way the *Rasā'il* can be considered 'a successful integration of Islam and Greek philosophy'.[5] Because of the contradictions the *Rasā'il* cannot be described as successfully integrating either of these central features of the medieval Middle East though, of all the influences and alien strands which compose the woof of the *Rasā'il*, the Greek may be said to predominate.

The tolerance of the Ikhwān should not be exaggerated or overemphasised. They could be arrogant towards, and sometimes intolerant of, those not possessed of their own truly astonishing intellectual and encyclopedic range, vitality and capacities. Thus their attitude towards the common people (*al-'āmma*) requires some clarification. Were the Ikhwān really a group which claimed to have a popular appeal, and which sought popular support, or were they elitists? They put themselves forward as the former in that they claimed to have infiltrated every sector of society, including the artisan class.[6] Yet this seems to be contradicted by the elitist attitudes which they adopted in connection with such subjects as magic, and their idea that the common people were fit only for the obvious or exoteric (*ẓāhir*) aspects of religion, such as knowledge of prayer and fasting.[7] The words 'common people' as used by the Ikhwān may sometimes have been a disparaging reference to those who did not attend their meetings (*majālis*) and were not members of, nor associated with, the Brethren. But it seems more likely that the contrast was between seekers of knowledge and the ignorant. The Ikhwān appealed popularly to those members of the populace who were willing to learn, and so used the term 'common people' (*al-'āmma*) derogatorily as a synonym for 'the ignorant' (*al-juhhāl*), giving the former word an intellectual rather than a purely class connotation. (Indeed, these same ignorant people are specified in some of their definitions of 'common people'.)[8]

What then were the Ikhwān? It is easy to state what they were not. They were not Ismā'īlīs; this is far too narrow a definition, besides being inaccurate. They were, however, influenced by Ismā'īlī thought. They have been described by some, like 'A. 'Awā, as encyclopedists, and, indeed, it is true that they had the encyclopedist's veneration for knowledge as well as his capacity to present a variegated and comprehensive survey of the learning of the age. But they were more than just scholars with a love of learning. Their relationship with Islam was uneasy to say the least, and their doctrine and philosophy, while embracing much of Islam, often transcended the individual Sunnī and Shī'ite branches of it. Yet to call them *un-Islamic* with no qualification would be to ignore the thoroughly Qur'ānic substrate of their writings as well as many other Islamic features in the *Rasā'il*.

Perhaps the most accurate definition is that they were Neoplatonic teachers intent on, and infatuated with, the propagation of a doctrine of purity, achieved through asceticism, self-denial, and righteous living, as a passport for entry to the Islamic Heaven. The pillars of this doctrine were tolerance, mutual help (*ta'āwun*) and a philosophy of eclecticism which utilised any text which might bolster their own teaching. The Brotherhood of Purity which they established was their 'Ship of Salvation'[9] from the sea of matter which included the world, its material aspects and a large number of its inhabitants. They were strenuously determined that they, and all whom they recruited to their Brotherhood, should not drown in this sea but should win eternal life and thereby free themselves finally from the bonds of matter and corruption and the prison house which was the world.

Notes

Bibliography

Index

Abbreviations

R. *Rasā'il Ikhwān al-Ṣafā'*, 4 vols (Beirut, Dār Ṣādir, 1957).

J. *al-Risālat al-Jāmi'a*, 2 vols, ed. by J. Salībā, (Damascus, al-Taraqqī Press, 1949).

Q. *Qur'ān*. Quotations are taken from A. J. Arberry's *The Koran Interpreted*, 2 vols (London, Allen & Unwin, 1955) using G. Flügel's numbering of verses.

EI2 *Encyclopaedia of Islam*, new ed., 4 vols completed, vol. 5 continuing; ed. by H. A. R. Gibb *et al.* (Leiden, E. J. Brill/ London, Luzac & Co., 1960–).

EIS *Shorter Encyclopaedia of Islam*, ed. by H. A. R. Gibb and J. H. Kramers (Leiden, E. J. Brill/London, Luzac & Co., 1961).

Notes

CHAPTER ONE

1 'Ārif Tāmir, *Ḥaqīqat Ikhwān al-Ṣafā' wa Khullān al-Wafā'* (Beirut, Imprimerie Catholique, 1966), p. 7.
2 A. L. Tibawi, 'Ikhwān aṣ-Ṣafā and their Rasā'il: a Critical Review of a Century and a Half of Research', *Islamic Quarterly*, vol. 2, no. 1 (1955), pp. 28–46.
3 e.g. R. 4, p. 283.
4 e.g. ibid., p. 5.
5 The confusion over the number of *Rasā'il* begins early: in the *Fihrist* at the beginning of the whole work, the number is given as 52: R. 1, p. 21.
6 R. 4, p. 284.
7 ibid., p. 283; Yves Marquet, 'Ikhwān al-Ṣafā'', *EI2*, vol. 3 p. 1073.
8 ibid.
9 Seyyed Hossein Nasr, *An Introduction to Islamic Cosmological Doctrines*, (Cambridge, Mass., Harvard University Press, 1964), p. 38.
10 R. 2, pp. 203–377.
11 *al-Risālat al-Jāmi'a*, 2 vols, ed. by J. Salībā (Damascus, al-Taraqqī Press, 1949).
12 Yves Marquet, 'Ikhwān al-Ṣafā'', p. 1075.
13 R. 1, pp. 42–3.
14 ibid., p. 42.
15 ibid., p. 46.
16 J. 2, p. 407.
17 Yves Marquet, 'Ikhwān al-Ṣafā'', p. 1075.
18 A. L. Tibawi, 'Ikhwān aṣ-Ṣafā and their Rasā'il', p. 37.
19 R. 4, pp. 41, 168.
20 J. 2, p. 395.
21 Aḥmad b. 'Alī al-Maqrīzī, *Kitāb al-Mawā'iz wa 'l-I'tibār bi-Dhikr al-Khiṭaṭ wa 'l-Āthār* (Baghdad, al-Muthannā, n.d.), vol. 1, p. 391.
22 For example R. 3, p. 107, R. 4, p. 120; A. L. Tibawi, 'Ikhwān aṣ-Ṣafā and their Rasā'il', p. 37.
23 See A. L. Tibawi, 'Ikhwān aṣ-Ṣafā and their Rasā'il', pp. 29, 37–39; Yves Marquet, 'Ikhwān al-Ṣafā'', p. 1071.
24 *al-Imtā' wa 'l-Mu'ānasa*, ed. by Aḥmad Amīn, (Beirut, Dār Maktabat al-Ḥayāt, n.d.) pt. 2, pp. 4–5; for a concise survey of these sources see Hossein Nasr, *Cosmological Doctrines*, pp. 25–6.
25 'The Authorship of the Epistles of the Ikhwān-aṣ-Ṣafā', *Islamic Culture* 20 (1946), pp. 367–72.
26 See A. L. Tibawi, 'Ikhwān aṣ-Ṣafā' and their Rasā'il'; Hossein Nasr, *Cosmological Doctrines*; 'A. 'Awā, *L'Esprit Critique des 'Frères de la Pureté': Encyclopédistes arabes du IVe/Xe siècle* (Beirut, Imprimerie Catholique, 1948); as an example of the continuing debate over the authorship, see Abbas Hamdani, 'Abū Ḥayyān al-Tawḥīdī and the Brethren of Purity', *International Journal of Middle East Studies* vol. 9, no. 3, (1978), pp. 345–53.
27 Hossein Nasr, *Cosmological Doctrines*, p. 35.
28 'Sur la date de la composition des "Rasā'il Ikhwān al ṣafa" ', *Der Islam* 4 (1913), p. 324.

29 'Une Date Astronomique dans les Épîtres des Ikhwān aṣ Ṣafā', *Journal Asiatique* 5 (1915), pp. 5–17.
30 A. L. Tibawi, 'Ikhwān aṣ-Ṣafā and their Rasā'il', p. 37.
31 ibid., pp. 28, 43–5.
32 *Āthār Ibn al-Muqaffa'*: *Kalīla wa Dimna* (Beirut, Dār Maktabat al-Ḥayāt, 1966), pp. 168–85. Hereafter this work is referred to simply as *Kalīla wa Dimna*.
33 R. 1, pp. 99–100.
34 'Über die Benennung der "Ichwān al-ṣafā" ', *Der Islam* 1 (1910), pp. 22–6.
35 *Kalīla wa Dimna*, p. 169; see R. 4, p. 41.
36 *Kalīla wa Dimna*, p. 182.
37 ibid., pp. 168, 185, 186.
38 R. 1, pp. 36, 39 (twice), 452; R. 4, p. 463.
39 R. 1, pp. 21, 43.
40 J. 1, p. 141.
41 R. 1, p. 47.
42 ibid., p. 361.
43 For example, ibid., pp. 21, 47.
44 R. A. Nicholson, *A Literary History of the Arabs* (Cambridge, Cambridge University Press, 1969), p. 370; W. Montgomery Watt, *Islamic Philosophy and Theology, Islamic Surveys 1* (Edinburgh, Edinburgh University Press, 1967), p. 102; M. Fakhry, *A History of Islamic Philosophy* (New York & London, Columbia University Press, 1970), pp. 185–202.
45 H. A. R. Gibb, *Arabic Literature*, 2nd rev. edn (Oxford, Clarendon Press, 1963), p. 99; G. E. Von Grunebaum, *Medieval Islam* (Chicago & London, University of Chicago Press, 1966), p. 317.
46 W. Montgomery Watt, *Islamic Philosophy and Theology*, p. 102.
47 G. E. Von Grunebaum, *Medieval Islam*, p. 40.
48 C. Brockelmann, *Geschichte der arabischen Litteratur* (Weimar, E. Felber, 1898), vol. 1, pp. 213–14.
49 ibid. (Leiden, E. J. Brill, 1943), vol. 1, p. 237; idem., *Erster Supplementband* (Leiden, E. J. Brill, 1937), p. 379.
50 G. Flügel, 'Über Inhalt und Verfasser der arabischen Encyclopädie *Rasā'il Ikhwān al-Ṣafā wa Khullān al-Wafā* d.i. die Abhandlungen der aufrichtigen Brüder und treuen Freunde', *Zeitschrift der Deutschen morgenländischen Gesellschaft* 13 (1859), pp. 1–43.
51 'A. 'Awā, op. cit.
52 J. 1, p. 717.
53 R. 4, p. 417.
54 ibid., pp. 411–12.
55 'Ikhwān aṣ-Ṣafā and their Rasā'il', p. 37.
56 Q. 111: 198–99; see also Q. 111: 109–10.
57 R. 4, pp. 41–2, 167.
58 R. 1, p. 38.
59 R. 4, p. 387.

CHAPTER TWO

1 G. S. Kirk and J. E. Raven, *The Presocratic Philosophers* (Cambridge, Cambridge University Press, 1962), p. 218.
2 *Metaphysics*, bk 1, 985b–986b.
3 ibid.
4 R. 1, p. 49.

5 R. 3, pp. 178–9.
6 ibid., pp. 178, 200; J. 1, pp. 29–30, 173.
7 R. 3, p. 200.
8 ibid., p. 180.
9 *Peri Tōn Pythagoreiōn* in *Aristotelis Fragmenta Selecta*, ed. by W. D. Ross (Oxford, Clarendon Press, 1955), pp. 138–9; an English translation of this appears in *Select Fragments*, ed. by W. D. Ross, *The Works of Aristotle Translated into English: vol. 12* (Oxford, Clarendon Press, 1952), p. 142.
10 *Metaphysics*, bk 1, 986a.
11 For example, 'Nay, by him that gave to our generation the tetractys, which contains the fount and root of eternal nature.' Kirk and Raven, op. cit., pp. 230–1; see also *Die Fragmente der Vorsokratiker*, ed. by H. Diels and W. Kranz (Berlin, Weidmann, 1951), vol. 1, pp. 454–5.
12 Diogenes Laertius, *Pythagoras* VIII:10 in *Lives of Eminent Philosophers*, trans. by R. D. Hicks, *Loeb Classical Library* (London, W. Heinemann/New York, G. P. Putnam's Sons, 1925), vol. 2, pp. 328–9.
13 R. 1, p. 49.
14 ibid., pp. 51–5.
15 ibid., pp. 116–17.
16 ibid., p. 213.
17 R. 3, pp. 183–4.
18 ibid., p. 474.
19 R. 4, p. 171.
20 ibid., p. 176.
21 R. 3, pp. 464–5.
22 Hossein Nasr, *Cosmological Doctrines*, pp. 77–8.
23 R. 1, pp. 52–3.
24 *Eclogae* in *Ioannis Stobaei Anthologium*, ed. by C. Wachsmuth and Otto Hense (Berlin, Weidmann, 1958), vol. 1, pp. 21–2.
25 J. 2, p. 295.
26 R. 3, pp. 181–2.
27 ibid., p. 179.
28 ibid., p. 182.
29 ibid., p. 200; J. 1, p. 173.
30 *Metaphysics*, bk 1, 987a–987b.
31 R. 1, pp. 49–50.
32 *Pythagoras and Early Pythagoreanism* (Toronto, University of Toronto Press, 1966), p. 125.
33 Aristotle, *On the Heavens*, bk 2, 290b.
34 R. 1, pp. 23, 206–8, 255, R. 3, pp. 94, 125.
35 *De Vita Pythagorica Liber* 15:64, 25:110–14, ed. by L. Deubner and U. Klein, (Stuttgart, B. G. Teubner, 1975), pp. 35–6, 63–5.
36 R. 1, pp. 185, 289.
37 R. 3, pp. 365, 370, 430; see Yves Marquet, 'Sabéens et Iḫwān al-Ṣafā'', *Studia Islamica* 24 (1966), pp. 74, 80. For a conflicting view see Geo Widengren, *The Gnostic Technical Language in the Rasā'il Iḫwān al-Ṣafā'* in *Actas Do IV Congresso De Estudos Arabes E Islâmicos: Coimbra-Lisboa 1968* (Leiden, E. J. Brill, 1971), p. 183. Widengren categorically states that in the *Rasā'il* 'the destiny of the human soul in spite of its eternal substance is transmigration'.
38 R. 4, p. 6.
39 See J. A. Philip, op. cit., pp. 39, 55.
40 R. 1, p. 300; see Manfred Ullmann, *Islamic Medicine, Islamic Surveys 11* (Edinburgh, Edinburgh University Press, 1978), pp. 57–60, and E. D. Phillips, *Greek Medicine* (London, Thames & Hudson, 1973), pp. 20–2, 48–52.

41 R. 2, p. 457.
42 ibid., p. 462.
43 ibid., p. 478.
44 ibid., *Risāla* 26: *On the Saying of the Sages that the Human is a Microcosm*, pp. 456–79.
45 Hossein Nasr, *Cosmological Doctrines*, pp. 96–104.
46 R. 2, p. 463; Hossein Nasr, *Cosmological Doctrines*, p. 100.
47 This Pythagorean work must be distinguished from the *Golden Epistle* attributed to Aristotle in which Aristotle replies to a letter from Alexander. The name *Golden Epistle* was also wrongly given to the spurious *De Mundo*. See F. E. Peters, *Aristoteles Arabus* (Leiden, E. J. Brill, 1968), pp. 61–2.
48 F. Rosenthal, 'Some Pythagorean Documents transmitted in Arabic', *Orientalia* 10 (1941), p. 105.
49 idem., 'Fīthāghūras', EI2, vol. 2, p. 929; this story is retailed, for example, by al-Nadīm, *Kitāb al-Fihrist*, (Teheran, Teheran Univeristy Press, 1971), p. 306; *Fihrist*, ed. and trans. by Bayard Dodge (New York and London, Columbia University Press, 1970), vol. 2, p. 590.
50 R. 4, pp. 36, 58, 175. Once, however, they call it *The Golden Exhortation* (*al-Waṣiyyat al-Dhahabiyya*): R. 1, p. 138.
51 F. Rosenthal, 'Fīthāghūras', p. 929.
52 R. 1, p. 138, R. 4, pp. 36, 58, 175.
53 A. Fabre d'Olivet, *The Golden Verses of Pythagoras*, trans. by N. L. Redfield (Wellingborough, Thorsons, 1975), pp. 8–9.
54 *The Republic* is referred to three times in the *Rasā'il* in a slightly different way each time: *Kitāb al-Siyāsa*: R. 4, p. 287; *al-Siyāsa*: R. 4, p. 288; *al-Siyāsāt*: R. 4, p. 306. The *Phaedo* dialogue is mentioned twice and again the Arabic rendering of the name varies: *Qādhūn*: R. 4, p. 304; and *Fādhan*: R. 4, p. 271.
55 *Phaedo*, 117A–118.
56 R. 4, pp. 287–8; the story is again alluded to in R. 4, p. 306. See *The Republic*, bk 2, 359–60.
57 R. 4, pp. 34–5, 73–4.
58 *Phaedo*, 64B–66E.
59 R. 4, p. 25; see also R. 3, p. 306, R. 4, p. 109.
60 R. 3, p. 65; see Muslim, *al-Jāmi' al-Ṣaḥīḥ: Kitāb al-Zuhd* (1), (Cairo, Dār al-Taḥrīr, 1964), pt 8, p. 210; al-Tirmidhī, *al-Jāmi' al-Ṣaḥīḥ: Kitāb al-Zuhd* (16), (Cairo, al-Ḥalabī, 1962), vol. 4, p. 562; Ibn Māja, *Sunan*: *Kitāb al-Zuhd* (3), (Cairo, Dār Iḥyā' al-Kutub al-'Arabiyya, 1954), vol. 2, p. 1378; Ibn Ḥanbal, *Musnad* (Beirut, Dār Ṣādir, n.d.), vol. 2, 197, 323, 389, 485.
61 R. 3, p. 49.
62 R. 4, p. 166; the *Jāmi'a* contains similar references to the bonds of nature and matter, e.g. J. 1, pp. 307, 500; J. 2, pp. 337, 351, 353, 397.
63 R. 2, pp. 458–9.
64 R. 4, p. 40.
65 Hossein Nasr, for example, noted (*Cosmological Doctrines*, pp. 102–3) that 'the soul of man, however, does not gain certainty and knowledge of things through these sense impressions, but only from the Intellect. In fact, the soul – as Plato asserts in the *Meno* – already possesses all knowledge in itself potentially. It only needs to recollect this knowledge, and the impression from the senses can do no more than to help in this recollection.' Nasr does not seem to have noted R. 3, p. 424, where it is made quite clear that there are three methods of acquiring knowledge of which a key one is sense perception. The use of the word 'recollection' implying the Platonic doctrine is unwarranted and misleading in this context. A. L. Tibawi ('Some Educational Terms in *Rasā'il Ikhwān aṣ-Ṣafā'*, *Islamic Quarterly*, vol. 5, nos. 1–2 (1959), p. 60) is another scholar who maintains that 'on the nature of the process of learning the *Rasā'il* claim to be based on Plato's doctrine that "learning is reminiscence" '.

66 See *Phaedo*, 72E ff.
67 R. 3, p. 424.
68 See Hilary Staniland, *Universals* (New York, Doubleday, 1972), p. IX.
69 R. 1, p. 238.
70 R. 2, p. 276.
71 For example, R. 4, pp. 418–19.
72 For example, R. 3, p. 8.
73 R. 4, pp. 34, 58, 73, 271; see *Phaedo*, 115–18.
74 R. 4, p. 35. For a description of the hierarchy of the Ikhwān, see p. 36.
75 R. 4, pp. 34–5, 73–4.
76 See F. E. Peters, *Aristotle and the Arabs* (New York, New York University Press/ London, University of London Press, 1968), p. 3. For a brief survey of Eastern and Western Aristotelianism, see the article 'Aristotelianism' by Ian R. Netton in *A Dictionary of Philosophy*, ed. by Antony Flew (London, Pan Books, 1979), pp. 21–3.
77 See A. E. Taylor, *Aristotle* (New York, Dover Publications/London, Constable, 1955), p. 37.
78 R. 4, p. 179.
79 The following correspondences, or partial correspondences, in title exist: *Categoriae*: *Risāla* 11; *De Interpretatione* or *Peri Herměneias*: *Risāla* 12; *Analytica Priora*: *Risāla* 13; *Analytica Posteriora*: *Risāla* 14; *De Caelo* and (doubtful Aristotle) *De Mundo*: *Risāla* 16; *De Generatione et Corruptione*: *Risāla* 17; *Meteorologica*: *Risāla* 18; *De Mineralibus* (spurious Aristotle): *Risāla* 19; *De Plantis* (doubtful Aristotle): *Risāla* 21; *De Partibus Animalium*, *Historia Animalium* and *De Generatione Animalium*: *Risāla* 22; *De Sensu et Sensibili*: *Risāla* 24; *De Anima*: *Risāla* 27; *De Longitudine et Brevitate Vitae*: *Risāla* 29.
80 R. 1, p. 268; see J. 1, pp. 225–6. I have followed 'Awā (op. cit., p. 152) and the editor of the *Jāmi'a* in reading *Bū'iṭīqā* instead of *Anūlūṭīqā* in the first definition, and *Anūlūṭīqā* instead of *Būlūṭīqā* (or *Yūlūṭīqā*: see R. 1, p. 203 in the 1928 Cairo ed of the *Rasā'il*) in the fourth.
81 R. 1, p. 269; see also ibid., p. 429.
82 *Categories*, 2a, lines 11ff.
83 *Metaphysics*, bk 5, 1017b; see also bk 7.
84 'The Conception of Substance in the Philosophy of the Ikhwan as-Safa' (*Brethren of Purity*)', *Medieval Studies* (Toronto) 5 (1943), p. 116.
85 R. 1, p. 401.
86 E. L. Fackenheim, op. cit., p. 117.
87 ibid., p. 116.
88 R. 3, p. 385.
89 R. 1, pp. 405–6.
90 E. L. Fackenheim, op. cit., pp. 116–18.
91 *Metaphysics* bk 7, 1029a.
92 R. 2, p. 6.
93 *Metaphysics*, bk 8, 1042a.
94 ibid., bk 7, 1029a. For a discussion of the relationship between matter and substance in the *Metaphysics* see Joseph Owens, *The Doctrine of Being in the Aristotelian 'Metaphysics'*, (Toronto, Pontifical Institute of Mediaeval Studies, 1963), pp. 330–45.
95 We may compare, for example, the definition of form in R. 2, p. 6, with that which appears in R. 3, p. 385, where form is defined as 'The essence of the thing (*māhiyyat al-shay'*) . . .'.
96 See 'Did Aristotle believe in Prime Matter?': appendix to *Aristotle's Physics: Books I and II*, trans. by W. Charlton, *Clarendon Aristotle Series* (Oxford, Clarendon Press, 1970), pp. 129–45.
97 R. 2, p. 6; R. 3, p. 184; Hossein Nasr, *Cosmological Doctrines*, pp. 58–9.

98 R. 2, p. 7.
99 ibid., p. 8.
100 R. 3, pp. 234–5.
101 A. E. Taylor, op. cit., p. 48.
102 *Metaphysics*, bk 9, 1048a.
103 R. 4, p. 122; see R. 3, p. 81.
104 R. 3, p. 47. In some of these examples, the word *nufūs*, which I have rendered as 'souls', could equally well be translated as 'minds'.
105 *Metaphysics*, bk 5, 1013a.
106 R. 2, p. 79; see ibid., p. 115, R. 3, p. 358.
107 R. 2, p. 79.
108 ibid., p. 89.
109 ibid., p. 155.
110 R. 3, p. 237.
111 R. 2, p. 89.
112 ibid., p. 155.
113 For this vocalisation see I. Goldziher/A. M. Goichon, 'Dahriyya, EI2, vol. 2, p. 95.
114 R. 3, p. 455.
115 R. 2, p. 12.
116 *Physics*, bk 4, 212a.
117 R. 2, p. 12.
118 ibid., p. 28; Aristotle wrote: '. . . it is clear that there is no such thing as a self-existing void' (*Physics*, bk 4, 216b).
119 R. 2, p. 28.
120 *Physics*, bk 4, 212a.
121 R. 3, p. 387.
122 See pp. 39, 118 n. 48.
123 R. 3, p. 352.
124 ibid.; Q. VII:52, Q. LVII:4; see Q. XXXII:4.
125 Q. XXII:46.
126 R. 3, p. 352.
127 ibid., p. 339.
128 ibid., pp. 340–1; see also ibid., pp. 19, 332, 520.
129 ibid., pp. 212–13.
130 ibid., p. 328.
131 R. 2, p. 18, J. 2, pp. 48–9; Hossein Nasr, *Cosmological Doctrines*, pp. 63–4; see also R. Arnaldez, 'Ḥaraka wa Sukūn', EI2, vol. 3, p. 171.
132 The Arabic words in brackets are those used by the Ikhwān for the ten categories. Other authors sometimes used different translations; for example Isḥāq b. Ḥunayn (d. 911) renders the categories of relation, posture or position, and possession or state as *iḍāfa*, *mawḍū'*, and *an yakūn lahu* respectively. See *Manṭiq Arisṭū*, ed. by 'A. R. Badawī (Cairo, Dār al-Kutub al-Miṣriyya, 1948), pt 1, p. 6.
133 *Risāla* 11: *On the Ten Words which are the Categories*: R. 1, pp. 404–13.
134 R. 1, p. 405.
135 ibid., pp. 405–6.
136 ibid., pp. 408–11.
137 ibid., p. 412; *Categories*, 14a–14b.
138 *Categories*, 15a.
139 *Risāla* 15: R. 11, p. 13.
140 *Risāla* 12: R. 1, pp. 414–19.
141 *Risāla* 13 and *Risāla* 14: R. 1, pp. 420–52.
142 R. 1, p. 423.
143 David Ross, *Aristotle* (London, Methuen, 1964), p. 33.
144 R. 1, pp. 439–40.

145 *Aristotle's Posterior Analytics*, trans. by J. Barnes, *Clarendon Aristotle Series* (Oxford, Clarendon Press, 1975), pp. X–XI.
146 *Posterior Analytics*, 71a; R. 1, p. 438.
147 R. 1, p. 429; note the use of the number four again.
148 ibid., pp. 430–1.
149 R. 1, p. 441; *Posterior Analytics*, 94a ff.
150 R. 1, p. 395; M. Fakhry, op. cit., pp. 188–9.
151 F. E. Peters, *Aristotle and the Arabs*, p. 131.
152 R. 2, pp. 184–5.
153 ibid., p. 196.
154 ibid., p. 192.
155 *Generation of Animals*, 733b; see also 780b ff., 761a ff.
156 M. Fakhry, op. cit., pp. 32ff.; see F. E. Peters, *Aristoteles Arabus*, pp. 72–4.
157 R. 1, p. 138, trans. by G. Lewis. His translation of the *Theologia Aristotelis* appears in *Plotini Opera*, 3 vols, ed. by P. Henry and H. R. Schwyzer (Paris, Desclée de Brouwer, 1951–73); see vol. 2, p. 225; vol. 3, p. 408.
158 R. 4, pp. 35, 271; see F. E. Peters, *Aristoteles Arabus*, pp. 65–6; D. Gutas, *Greek Wisdom Literature in Arabic Translation: a Study of the Graeco-Arabic Gnomologia* (New Haven, American Oriental Society, 1975), pp. 425–26; George N. Atiyeh, *al-Kindī: the Philosopher of the Arabs* (Rawalpindi, Islamic Research Institute, 1966), pp. 158–9; J. Kraemer, 'Das arabische Original des Pseudo-Aristotelischen *Liber de Pomo*' in *Studi Orientalistici in onore di Giorgio Levi della Vida* (Rome, Istituto per l'Oriente, 1956), vol. 1, pp. 484–506; D. S. Margoliouth, 'The Book of the Apple, ascribed to Aristotle' (ed. in Persian and English), *Journal of the Royal Asiatic Society* (1892), pp. 187–92, 202–52.
159 By A. L. Tibawi, 'Ikhwān aṣ-Ṣafā and their Rasā'il', p. 44.
160 I. R. al-Fārūqī, 'On the Ethics of the Brethren of Purity', *Muslim World* 50 (April 1960), p. 116; (October 1960), p. 254.

CHAPTER THREE

1 R. T. Wallis, *Neoplatonism* (London, Duckworth, 1972), pp. 160–3.
2 A. H. Armstrong, 'Plotinus' in *The Cambridge History of Later Greek and Early Medieval Philosophy*, ed. by A. H. Armstrong (Cambridge, Cambridge University Press, 1967), p. 195.
3 R. T. Wallis, op. cit., p. 37.
4 *Enneads* V, 1, 10: *Plotini Opera*, 3 vols, ed. by P. Henry and H. R. Schwyzer, (Paris, Desclée de Brouwer, 1951–73). Standard translations include those by S. MacKenna (London, Faber & Faber, 2nd ed 1956) and A. H. Armstrong (*Loeb Classical Library*, London, W. Heinemann/Cambridge, Mass., Harvard University Press, 1966–67). The latter, in 3 vols, is complete to the end of the third *Ennead*.
5 *Enneads* V, 1, 8.
6 ibid., V, 1, 6.
7 ibid., IV, 5, 6–7; R. T. Wallis, op. cit., p. 61.
8 R. 1, p. 53.
9 ibid., p. 54; see also R. 3, pp. 184, 196–7, 235.
10 *Enneads* I, 8, 14.
11 *De Malorum Subsistentia* in *Tria Opuscula*, ed. by H. Boese (Berlin, W. de Gruyter, 1960), pp. 172–4, 208–22; R. T. Wallis, op. cit., p. 157.
12 Hossein Nasr, *Cosmological Doctrines*, p. 58.
13 R. 3, pp. 196–7.
14 *Enneads* III, 2, 2.

15 R. 3, p. 338.
16 ibid., pp. 56, 181–2.
17 ibid., pp. 203–4.
18 See R. T. Wallis, op. cit., pp. 118–34, 146–59.
19 'A. 'Awā, op. cit., pp. 289–90; Yves Marquet, 'Imamat, Résurrection et Hiérarchie selon les Ikhwan as-Safa', *Revue des Études Islamiques* 30 (1962), p. 103.
20 R. 4, pp. 57–8, 174–5. Hossein Nasr (*Cosmological Doctrines*, p. 32 n. 34) rightly warns that such arbitrary ages should not be interpreted too literally. Jesus, for example, did not reach the age of fifty.
21 ibid., p. 230.
22 ibid., pp. 276–81.
23 ibid., pp. 176–7.
24 R. 1, p. 311.
25 ibid., p. 406.
26 R. 3, p. 123.
27 R. 4, p. 123.
28 R. 1, pp. 408–9.
29 For a concise survey of the differences between a *theos* and a *daimōn*, see art. 'Daimon' in *The Oxford Classical Dictionary*, 2nd ed, ed. by N. G. L. Hammond and H. H. Scullard (Oxford, Clarendon Press, 1970), p. 310.
30 See *Enneads* V, 4, 1.
31 Yves Marquet, 'Ikhwān al-Ṣafā'', p. 1073.
32 S. MacKenna, op. cit., p. XXIV.
33 R. 3, p. 184.
34 R. 1, p. 54.
35 R. 2, p. 128.
36 See *Enneads* VI, 7, 34.
37 Q. LXXXIX: 28.
38 R. 2, p. 139; 'A. 'Awā, op. cit., p. 173.
39 For example, R. 4, pp. 40, 462.
40 R. 1, p. 451.
41 R. 3, p. 328.
42 ibid., p. 285.
43 ibid., pp. 403, 515; see R. 4, pp. 206–8; see also 'A. 'Awā, op. cit., p. 191.
44 See M. A. Shaban, *Islamic History: a New Interpretation 2:* A.D. *750–1055* (A.H. *132–448*), (Cambridge, Cambridge University Press, 1976), pp. 54–5.
45 See 'A. 'Awā, op. cit., pp. 183–92.
46 Yves Marquet, *La Philosophie des Iḫwān al-Ṣafā'* (Algiers, Société Nationale d'Édition et de Diffusion, 1975), p. 60; idem, 'Coran et Création', *Arabica* vol. 11, no. 3 (1964), p. 279.
47 R. 3, p. 517. See 'A. 'Awā, op. cit., pp. 187–8.
48 ibid.; see Yves Marquet, *La Philosophie des Iḫwān al-Ṣafā'*, p. 60. The Ikhwān carefully distinguished between the similar verbs *khalaqa* and *ṣana'a* on the one hand and *abda'a* and *ikhtara'a* on the other. They reserved the first to indicate creation out of something else while the second merely referred to the presence of form in matter. The third and fourth, however, bore the connotation of creation *ex nihilo* (R. 3, pp. 472–3).
49 An essentially Mu'tazilite term: see 'A. 'Awā, op. cit., p. 165.
50 R. 3, p. 518; 'A. 'Awā, op. cit., pp. 190–1.
51 R. 3, p. 338.
52 ibid., p. 518.
53 ibid., p. 515. Here the Ikhwān specify that 'the common people (*al-'āmma*)' consist of women, youths and the ignorant, and they link them with those who know nothing of the mathematical, physical, rational and divine sciences. Thus the word *al-'āmma*

is here equated more with those who lack knowledge rather than used to designate a particular class of people. The same definition of *al-'āmma* as 'women, youths and the ignorant' appears in R. 3, p. 511, where they are contrasted with *al-khāṣṣa*, the specialists or experts who are distinguished for their knowledge. See M. G. S. Hodgson, 'Bāṭiniyya', EI2, vol. 1, p. 1099.

54 R. 4, p. 208.
55 'A. 'Awā, op. cit., pp. 191–2.
56 See Hossein Nasr, *Cosmological Doctrines*, p. 53; E. L. Fackenheim, op. cit., p. 117.
57 R. 3, p. 290.
58 ibid., p. 285.
59 ibid., p. 414.
60 R. 4, pp. 62–3.
61 ibid., pp. 63–4.
62 ibid., p. 165.
63 R. 3, p. 452.
64 R. 4, p. 158.
65 See I. R. al-Fārūqī, op. cit. (April 1960), p. 115; R. 2, p. 384.
66 R. 2, p. 17, R. 4, p. 305.
67 R. 4, p. 131.
68 R. 3, p. 453.
69 Q. XLII:50–1; R. 4, p. 84.
70 Q. IV:144; R. 4, p. 133.
71 A. L. Tibawi, 'The Idea of Guidance in Islam from an Educational Point of View', *Islamic Quarterly* vol. 3, no. 2 (1956), p. 139.
72 R. 4, p. 40.
73 ibid., p. 126.
74 ibid., p. 48.
75 ibid., p. 387.
76 Hossein Nasr, *Cosmological Doctrines*, pp. 55–6.
77 *Enneads* III, 8, 11.
78 R. 3, pp. 285–6; see L. A. Giffen, *Theory of Profane Love among the Arabs: The Development of the Genre* (New York, New York University Press/London, University of London Press, 1971–2), pp. 143–4.
79 J. 1, p. 277; Hossein Nasr, *Cosmological Doctrines*, pp. 53–6.
80 R. 3, p. 185; 'A. 'Awā, op. cit., p. 164.
81 J. 2, p. 33.
82 Hossein Nasr, *Cosmological Doctrines*, p. 56; R. 3, p. 184.
83 A. H. Armstrong, *Cambridge History*, p. 250.
84 R. 3, p. 290.
85 See Hossein Nasr, *Cosmological Doctrines*, pp. 56–7.
86 R. 3, p. 328, R. 4, p. 340; see *Enneads*, V, 1, 2.
87 R. 3, pp. 185, 238.
88 IV, 3, 32; R. T. Wallis, op. cit., p. 73.
89 III, 4, 2.
90 R. 1, pp. 311–12.
91 Hossein Nasr, *Cosmological Doctrines*, p. 65, n. 77.
92 R. T. Wallis, op. cit., p. 73.
93 E. L. Fackenheim, op. cit., pp. 115–16.
94 R. 3, p. 385.
95 E. L. Fackenheim, op. cit., p. 117.
96 M. Fakhry, op. cit., pp. 68–9, 237–8.
97 R. 1, pp. 401, 405.
98 R. 2, p. 53.
99 R. 3, pp. 235–6.

100 R. 1, pp. 408–9.
101 T. J. de Boer, *The History of Philosophy in Islam* (London, Luzac & Co., 1970), p. 91.
102 *Isagoge sive quinque voces* in *Porphyrii Isagoge et in Aristotelis Categorias Commentarium*, ed. by A. Busse, *Commentaria in Aristotelem Graeca 4, 1* (Berlin, G. Reimer, 1887); *Risāla* 10: *On the Eisagōgē*: R. 1, pp. 390–403.
103 R. Walzer, 'Furfūriyūs', EI2, vol. 2, p. 948.
104 Yves Marquet, 'Ikhwān al-Ṣafā', p. 1075.
105 For example R. 1, pp. 266, 269; R. 3, p. 436.
106 Claudius Ptolemaeus (*c.* AD 150) tried to systematise the attempts of Greeks before him to explain planetary motion in a treatise which became known as the *Almagest* from its Arabic title *al-Mijisṭī*. He and the *Almagest* are referred to many times in the *Rasā'il*, for example R. 1, pp. 138, 169, 208, 437; R. 2, pp, 288, 399; R. 3, pp. 94, 209, 256, 259, 303, 323, 326, 332, 335, 438, 471; R. 4, pp. 285, 338, 360, 382; J. 2, p. 99.
107 R. 1, p. 24.
108 ibid., p. 269.
109 ibid., p. 391.
110 ibid., p. 395.
111 M. Fakhry, op. cit., p. 189; see *Rasā'il al-Kindī al-Falsafiyya*, ed. by M. A. Abū Rīdah (Cairo, Dār al-Fikr al-'Arabī, 1950), vol. 1, pp. 126–7.
112 George N. Atiyeh, op. cit., p. 36.
113 See the edition of G. Van Vloten (Leiden, E. J. Brill, 1895), p. 141.
114 'A. 'Awā, op. cit., pp. 154–5; T. J. de Boer, op. cit., p. 89.
115 R. T. Wallis, op. cit., pp. 90–3.
116 R. 3, pp. 517–18, 498, 493.
117 ibid., pp. 520–7.
118 R. T. Wallis, op. cit., p. 7.
119 R. 3, p. 8.
120 See *Enneads*, I, 3.
121 ibid., VI, 7, 36.
122 ibid., VI, 9, 10.
123 *Vita Plotini* 23 in *Plotini Opera*, vol. 1; trans. by S. MacKenna in op. cit., p. 17.
124 R. 4, p. 58.
125 R. 2, p. 376.
126 Hossein Nasr, *Cosmological Doctrines*, pp. 31, 36, 53; see R. 1, p. 137, and *Risāla 37*: *On the Essence of Passion (al-'Ishq)*: R. 3, pp. 269–86.
127 R. 1, p. 377; the *Abdāl* occupied fifth place in the Ṣūfī hierarchy of saints and helped to maintain the order of the cosmos. See I. Goldziher, 'Abdāl', EI2, vol. 1 pp. 94–5.
128 R. 1, p. 240.
129 See M. Plessner, 'Hirmis', EI2, vol. 3, pp. 463–5; G. Vajda, 'Idrīs', in ibid., pp. 1030–1; see also *Corpus Hermeticum*, 4 vols, ed. by A. D. Nock and A. J. Festugière (Paris, Société d'Édition 'Les Belles Lettres', 1972); *Hermetica*, 4 vols, ed. by Walter Scott (London, Dawsons of Pall Mall, 1968).
130 R. 1, p. 138; R. 4, p. 445. See also R. 1, pp. 225–6, where he is called 'the third in wisdom (*al-thālith bi 'l-ḥikma*)'.
131 Or astonomy. The Arabic '*Ilm al-Nujūm* means both. R. 1, p. 138; see R. 3, p. 502.
132 R. 4, pp. 443 ff.
133 R. 1, p. 297.
134 R. 2, p. 231. The name Hermes does not appear in the Qur'ān but Idrīs does: Q. XIX:57–8, Q. XXI:85–6.
135 R. 4, p. 367.
136 R. 1, p. 145, R. 4, p. 285; see also R. 3, p. 500.
137 R. 4, p. 285; see R. 2, p. 450, R. 3, p. 500.
138 R. 4, pp. 217 ff.

139 R. 1, p. 142.
140 See R. 2, pp. 418, 421, 446; R. 4, p. 390.
141 R. 4, pp. 388–9, 401, 406.
142 R. 1, pp. 153–5.
143 R. 3, p. 499; M. Fakhry, op. cit., p. 204.
144 See Macrobius, *Saturnalia*, 1:19 (Leipzig, B. G. Teubner, 1963), vol. 1; there is a translation by P. V. Davies (New York and London, Columbia University Press, 1969), p. 135.
145 R. 4, p. 445; the work is more commonly vowelled as *al-Usṭūṭās*. See M. Plessner, 'Hermes Trismegistus and Arab Science', *Studia Islamica* 2 (1954), p. 58, n. 2, and Yves Marquet, *La Philosophie des Iḫwān al-Ṣafā'*, p. 125, n. 110.
146 R. 4, pp. 428–46; Yves Marquet, *La Philosophie des Iḫwān al-Ṣafā'*, pp. 125, 130, 143–4; see also idem, 'Imamat', pp. 139–42.
147 See B. Carra de Vaux, 'al-Ṣābi'a', EIS, pp. 477–8.
148 Yves Marquet, 'Sabéens et Iḫwān al-Ṣafā'', pp. 62, 80.
149 S. Lane-Poole, *Studies in a Mosque, Khayats Oriental Reprint No. 21* (Beirut, Khayats, 1966), p. 206.

CHAPTER FOUR

1 See G. Parrinder, *Jesus in the Qur'ān* (London, Faber & Faber, 1965), pp. 43, 155.
2 Exodus 3:6.
3 For example Matthew 5:17, John 8:56.
4 Galatians 3:29.
5 Q. III:60, Q. II:121.
6 R. 4, p. 126.
7 Q. II:124; R. 1, p. 76.
8 See A. Guillaume, *The Traditions of Islam, Khayats Oriental Reprint No. 13* (Beirut, Khayats, 1966), pp. 132–49; Ignaz Goldziher, *Muslim Studies*, trans. by C. R. Barber and S. M. Stern, (London, Allen & Unwin, 1971), vol. 2, pp. 346–62.
9 For example S. Lane-Poole (op. cit., p. 196) observed: 'They knew, too, the Old and New Testaments well enough to correct the mistakes of the Korān; and their story of the Messiah is said to be "the worthiest record of the life of Jesus that can be met with in Arabic literature" '; see also 'A. 'Awā, op. cit., p. 306; M. Fakhry, op. cit., p. 203; Buṭrus al-Bustānī in his Introduction to the *Rasā'il*: R. 1, p. 11 (1957 edn).
10 R. 4, p. 245.
11 See B. Carra de Vaux/G. C. Anawati, 'Indjīl', EI2, vol. 3, pp. 1205–8.
12 R. 1, p. 144.
13 R. 2, p. 280.
14 e.g. ibid., p. 232.
15 e.g. R. 3, p. 207; also rendered as *al-Aysū'* (R. 4, p. 19).
16 e.g. R. 2, p. 280.
17 R. 4, p. 19.
18 e.g. ibid., p. 42.
19 R. 1, p. 363.
20 R. 3, p. 246.
21 R. 2, pp. 283–4; see J. 2, p. 150. Compare Q. II:81, 254, Q. XXI:91; Matthew 1:18–23.
22 For an excellent discussion of these sects see J. N. D. Kelly, *Early Christian Doctrines*, 5th rev. edn, (London, A. & C. Black, 1977), pp. 310–43. Some Monophysites were called Jacobites after the Monophysite bishop James Baradai (d. 578) and it is as *Ya'qūbī* or *Ya'qūbiyya* that the Ikhwān refer to them (R. 2, p. 367, R. 3, p. 161).

23 See J. W. Sweetman, *Islam and Christian Theology* (London, Lutterworth Press, 1945), pt 1, vol. 1, p. 39. The Syriac words *'nāšūthā* and *'alāhūthā* were *general* terms for humanity and divinity used in both Monophysite and Nestorian texts, e.g. Philoxenus of Mabbug, *Tractatus Tres de Trinitate et Incarnatione*, ed. and trans. by A. Vaschalde, *Corpus Scriptorum Christianorum Orientalium vols 9, 10, Scriptores Syri vols 9, 10* (Reprinted Louvain, Secrétariat du Corpus SCO, 1955, 1961), vol. 9, p. 35, vol. 10, p. 32; *A Nestorian Collection of Christological Texts: Cambridge University Library MS. Oriental 1319*, ed. and trans. by L. Abramowski and A. E. Goodman (Cambridge, Cambridge University Press, 1972), vol. 1, p. 4, vol. 2, p. 5. The more specific Syriac word used to render 'nature' (Greek: *phusis*), divine or human, was *kyānā*, e.g. Philoxenus, op. cit., vol. 9, p. 34, vol. 10, p. 31. For Ṣūfism see John A. Subhan, *Sufism: its Saints and Shrines* (New York, Samuel Weiser, 1970), pp. 24, 75; al-Ḥusayn b. Manṣūr al-Ḥallāj, *Akhbār al-Ḥallāj*, publié, annoté et traduit par L. Massignon and P. Kraus, (Paris, Editions-Larose, 1936), pp. 8, 83.

24 R. 2, 367; R. 3, p. 161.

25 See Q. II:81; W. Montgomery Watt, *Companion to the Qur'ān* (London, Allen & Unwin, 1967), p. 24; G. Parrinder, op. cit., pp. 48–51.

26 J. 2, pp. 150, 362; G. Parrinder, op. cit., pp. 78–9; see Q. III:41, Q. V:10, Q. XIX:30–4; M. R. James, *The Apocryphal New Testament* (Oxford, Clarendon Press, 1924, reprinted 1975), pp. 80–2; P. Peeters, *Évangiles Apocryphes* (Paris, A. Picard, 1914), vol. 2, p. 1; E. Hennecke, *New Testament Apocrypha*, ed. by W. Schneemelcher (London, Lutterworth Press, 1963), vol. 1, pp. 408–9; Ibn Hishām, *al-Sīrat al-Nabawiyya*, ed. by M. Saqqā *et al.* (Cairo, al-Ḥalabī, 1955), vol. 1, p. 575; trans. by A. Guillaume, *The Life of Muhammad. A Translation of Isḥāq's Sīrat Rasūl Allāh* (O.U.P. Pakistan Branch, 1955), p. 271.

27 R. 4, p. 16; compare Luke 2:41–50.

28 R. 4, pp. 29–30; compare Matthew 4:18–20.

29 R. 2, p. 284.

30 R. 4, p. 30; compare Matthew 9:35.

31 R. 4, pp. 28–31, 425, R. 3, p. 485; compare Luke 7:18–23.

32 See A. Guillaume, *The Traditions of Islam*, p. 138; N. Daniel, *Islam and the West* (Edinburgh, Edinburgh University Press, 1966), pp. 73–7.

33 e.g. Mark 8:11–13.

34 Q. V:110–15; compare R. 3, p. 485.

35 Ibn Hishām, op. cit., p. 575; A. Guillaume, *The Life of Muhammad*, p. 271.

36 R. 3, p. 485. The more metaphysical account in the *Rasā'il* in which spiritual blindness is cured may be compared with the physical healing by Jesus in John 9:6–7.

37 Luke 19:41–4.

38 R. 4, pp. 28–9; compare Matthew 9:36.

39 R. 4, p. 29; compare Mark 4:2.

40 J. 1, p. 373.

41 R. 4, pp. 29–30.

42 *The Gospel of Philip*, trans. from the Coptic text by R. McL. Wilson, (London, A. R. Mowbray & Co., 1962), p. 39; see also p. 37. The Coptic text appears in *L'Évangile selon Philippe*, ed. and trans. by J. E. Ménard, (Paris, Letouzey & Ané, 1967), pp. 70–1.

43 Matthew 23:27–8.

44 R. 4, p. 29.

45 Mark 9:3; see also Revelation 7:14, in which robes are washed white in the blood of the Lamb; Exodus 19:10–14, where the people of Israel are commanded to wash their garments in preparation for God's descent upon Mt Sinai; Zechariah 3:3–5, where Joshua's dirty garments, representing sin, are replaced with clean ones; Malachi 3:2, where God is compared to the soap of the fuller.

46 R. 3, pp. 77–8; compare Matthew 13:11.

47 Matthew 21:19.
48 Q. XXVII:20 ff.
49 The Ikhwān seem to have had a preference for the Gospel of St John: Yves Marquet, *La Philosophie des Iḫwān al-Ṣafā'*, p. 354 n. 256; the *Rasā'il* version of Christ's passion has been translated by L. Levonian ('The Ikhwān al-Ṣafā' and Christ', *Muslim World* 35 (1945), pp. 27–31) and J. W. Sweetman (op. cit., pp. 38–9).
50 R. 4, p. 30; compare Luke 13:31 and John 11:53–54.
51 R. 4, p. 74; compare Philippians 2:7–8.
52 R. 4, pp. 30–1; compare John 13:1; Matthew 26:18–19, Mark 14:14–16, Luke 22:10–12; John 14:12, 28, John 16:10, 28.
53 Q. III:48.
54 Matthew 12:30; R. 4, p. 31.
55 R. 4, p. 31; compare Matthew 28:19, Mark 16:15, Acts 1:8; Matthew 10:28; Psalms 110:1, Mark 16:19; John 20:17; Matthew 18:20. This covenant in the *Rasā'il* may also be compared with that made by God with His Prophets in Q. III:75.
56 See Q. IX:72, Q. III:100, Q. VII:156.
57 R. 4, p. 31; compare Matthew 23:34, Luke 11:49–50.
58 R. 4, p. 31; compare Matthew 26:50, Luke 22:54, John 18:12; John 19:16.
59 R. 4, p. 31; compare particularly John 19 and Matthew 27–8.
60 'Abd al-Tafāhum, 'Doctrine' in *Religion in the Middle East*, ed. by A. J. Arberry *et al.* (Cambridge, Cambridge University Press, 1969), vol. 2, p. 397; R. 2, p. 284.
61 M. Fakhry, op. cit., p. 203; J. W. Sweetman, op. cit., p. 40.
62 However, the Ikhwān's views appear less unorthodox if we accept Parrinder's arguments that 'the cumulative effect of the Quranic verses is strongly in favour of a real death, and a complete self-surrender of Jesus' (op. cit., p. 121) and that 'Docetic influence on the Qur'ān is not proved' (ibid., p. 119).
63 Q. XIX:20–30.
64 Q. V:19.
65 Q. III:48.
66 Q. IV:156.
67 The translation of this phrase has given rise to some difficulty: J. Platts, in his translation of the Debate from the Urdu, refers to this character as 'The Enterpriser' (*Ikhwanu-Ṣ-Ṣafā; or, Brothers of Purity* (London, W. H. Allen, 1875), pp. 40, 129). Yves Marquet corrects a previous rendering, 'Le maître de la sorcellerie (des djinns)', to 'L'Inflexible' ('Révélation et Vision Véridique chez les Ikhwān al-Safā'', *Revue des Études Islamiques* 32 (1964), p. 27.)
68 R. 2, p. 284.
69 ibid., p. 218.
70 R. 3, p. 72.
71 ibid., p. 523.
72 L. Gardet, 'Djanna', EI2, vol. 2, p. 449.
73 Q. LXXVI:12–15.
74 R. 3, p. 78.
75 R. 4, p. 30.
76 My italics. R. 3, p. 77.
77 ibid., p. 72.
78 John 3:3.
79 R. 1, p. 226.
80 R. 2, p. 443; J. 1, p. 562.
81 R. 2, p. 443.
82 See p. 59; R. 4, p. 31.
83 R. 1, p. 138, R. 4, pp. 58, 175.
84 R. 4, p. 165.
85 For New Testament references see n. 55 of these notes, above.

86 R. 4, p. 175; compare 'My Father and your Father' here with John 20:17 and also Q. V:117, Q. XIX:37 ('My Lord and your Lord') and Q. XXIX:45 ('Our God and your God').

87 Q. V:118; R. 1, p. 372, R. 3, p. 313; J. 2, p. 224.

88 Q. V:116; J. 2, pp. 193, 221; see Q. V:19.

89 J. 2, pp. 221–2: not all these phrases occur in every manuscript as Salībā shows. See J. 1, p. 632, where the seventh leader is called 'the Lord [or Chief] (*Sayyid*) of Ikhwān al-Ṣafā''.

90 Q. V:116; J. 2, p. 222.

91 J. 2, p. 364. The image probably derives ultimately from the Qur'ān, see Q. XXIII:14.

92 R. 2, pp. 368–9, R. 1, p. 375.

93 John 6:66–8.

94 See Q. III:45, Q. LXI:14. Both Q. III:45 and John 6:65–6 stress the unbelief perceived by Jesus in some of His followers before He asks His question in each case.

95 Matthew 10:38–9, Matthew 16:24–5, Mark 8:34–5, Luke 9:23–4, Luke 14:27, John 12:25–6; Matthew 10:17–18, Matthew 24:9, John 16:2.

96 R. 4, pp. 122, 166.

97 Q. III:43, Q. V:110, Q. XLIII:63. See A. M. Goichon, 'Ḥikma', EI2, vol. 3, p. 377.

98 Matthew 7:6.

99 R. 1, p. 349; compare Q. VII:84.

100 R. 3, p. 15.

101 Matthew 19:24, Mark 10:25, Luke 18:25.

102 R. 1, p. 226; Q. VII:38. There is some ambiguity here involved in the Arabic word used for 'camel' (*jamal*). *Jamal* can also mean 'ship's cable' (*ḥabl al-safina*) and this meaning is specified by the editor of the 1957 edn of the *Rasā'il* in a footnote (R. 1, p. 226). E. W. Lane translates the Qur'ānic phrase as: 'until the cable shall enter into the eye of the needle" (*An Arabic–English Lexicon* (Beirut, Librairie du Liban, reprinted 1968), vol. 2, p. 461); W. Montgomery Watt notes that this possibility has been mentioned by both Muslim and Christian commentators and that 'needle' may also signify 'a small side-gate' (*Companion to the Qur'ān*, p. 89). See also the same author's article 'The Camel and the Needle's Eye' in *Ex Orbe Religionum: Studia Geo Widengren Oblata*, ed. by C. J. Bleeker *et al.*, *Studies in the History of Religions XXII*, (Leiden, E. J. Brill, 1972), vol. 2, pp. 155–8. Whatever the ambiguity in the Arabic, however, modern New Testament scholarship is agreed that the phrase should be understood *literally* as a hyperbole; for example 'Procrustean attempts to reduce the camel to a rope (reading *kámilon* for *kámēlon*) or to enlarge the needle's eye into a postern gate need not be taken seriously' (C. E. B. Cranfield, *The Gospel According to Saint Mark: an Introduction and Commentary* (Cambridge, Cambridge University Press, 1959), p. 332).

103 R. 3, pp. 6, 77, 82, 516; R. 4, p. 235; J. 1, pp. 90–1, 134, 183, 516, 693, 695; J. 2, pp. 15, 209; see Isaiah 64:4, 1 Corinthians 2:9; compare Q. XXXII:17. Most compilers of *ḥadīth* include the phrase in their collections, e.g. al-Bukhārī, *Ṣaḥīḥ: Kitāb Bad' al-Khalq* (Cairo, al-Ḥalabī, 1926), pt 4, p. 143. For a full survey of *ḥadīth* references see William A. Graham, *Divine Word and Prophetic Word in Early Islam* (The Hague, Mouton, 1977), pp. 117–18.

104 L. Gardet, op. cit., p. 451; see Rashīd Riḍā, *Fatāwā* (Beirut, Dār al-Kitāb al-Jadīd, 1970), vol. 2, p. 513.

105 *The Gospel according to Thomas*, Coptic text estab. and trans. by A. Guillaumont, H.-Ch. Puech *et al.*, (Leiden, E. J. Brill/London, Collins, 1959), p. 13.

106 R. 2, p. 284.

107 Q. V:77. G. Parrinder (op. cit., p. 134) does not see this Qur'ānic verse as a denial of Christian doctrine if it is taken as a reference to three Gods, for Christianity does not believe in three Gods any more than Islam.

108 R. 1, p. 217.
109 R. 4, p. 175.
110 R. 1, p. 138; see R. 4, p. 19.
111 Q. IV:169.
112 J. 1, p. 539.
113 But see W. Montgomery Watt, *Islamic Philosophy and Theology*, pp. 65–6.
114 R. 3, p. 523.
115 J. 2, p. 139.
116 R. 3, p. 86; R. 1, p. 27.
117 J. 1, p. 103.
118 R. 1, p. 40; J. 2, pp. 354, 365.
119 R. 1, p. 40; J. 2, p. 365.
120 J. 2, p. 354: a very Ismā'īlī designation.
121 ibid.
122 See Q. LXI:6; G. Parrinder, op. cit., pp. 96–100; J. Schacht, 'Aḥmad', EI2, vol. 1, p. 267.
123 For example Q. IV:15, 116, Q. LX:12.
124 Q. VII:20–5.
125 ibid., v. 24.
126 Romans 5:12.
127 R. 4, p. 160.
128 R. 1, p. 100; see also R. 2, p. 21, R. 4, p. 166.
129 R. 1, p. 100, R. 2, p. 21.
130 R. 3, p. 163, R. 4, pp. 87–8. The following clerical ranks are mentioned: Catholicos (Arabic *Jāthilīq* from Greek *Katholikos*), a title borne by the primates of the Armenian, Georgian and Nestorian Churches; Metropolitan Archbishop (Arabic *Muṭrān* from Greek *Mētropolitēs*); priest (Arabic *Qissīs* from Syriac *Qaššīšā*); deacon (Arabic *Shammās* from Syriac *Šammāšā*).
131 For example see his *'al-Radd 'alā 'l-Naṣārā'* in *Thalāth Rasā'il*, ed. by J. Finkel (Cairo, Salafiyya Press, 1926), pp. 9–38; trans. by I. S. Allouche, 'Un Traité de Polémique Christiano–Musulmane au IXe Siècle', *Hesperis* 26 (1939), pp. 123–55.
132 R. 4, p. 245.
133 Q. II:59; see also Q. V:73; R. 4, p. 121.
134 R. 2, pp. 231–2.
135 ibid., p. 307.
136 ibid., pp. 206–7.
137 R. 1, p. 359.
138 R. 4, pp. 255, 54; see Acts 2:44–5, Acts 4:32–7.
139 R. 1, p. 156.
140 Compare Q. V:85 with Q. IX:34.
141 op. cit, p. 164.
142 *The Traditions of Islam*, p. 142.
143 R. 3, p. 8.
144 R. 2, p. 376.
145 R. 1, pp. 338–42.
146 R. 4, p. 32.
147 For example R. 1, p. 363.
148 R. 4, p. 306.
149 R. 2, p. 218.
150 Deuteronomy 14:7–8.
151 R. 2, p. 288.
152 ibid., p. 283; Q. V:65; see Q. IV:54. J. W. Sweetman (op. cit., p. 35) believes that the word *Ṭāghūt* probably has a Talmudic origin.
153 R. 2, pp. 324–5.

154 Q. IX:30.
155 R. Paret, 'Ibrāhīm', EI2, vol. 3, p. 981.
156 R. 4, pp. 291–2.
157 Q. II:260; see also Q. XXI:68, Q. XXIX:23, Q. XXXVII:95; al-Ṭabarī, *Jāmi' al-Bayān 'an Ta'wīl Āy al-Qur'ān*, 2nd edn (Cairo, al-Ḥalabī, 1954), pt 3, pp. 23–4.
158 Genesis 10:9.
159 *Genesis Rabbah* LXIII:13 on Genesis 25:32: *Midrash Rabbah: Genesis 2*, ed. by H. Freedman and M. Simon (London, Soncino Press, 1961).
160 *Pirḳê De Rabbi Eliezer* 24, ed. and trans. by Gerald Friedlander (New York, Hermon Press, 1970 (Reprint of London, Kegan Paul, 1916 edn)), pp. 175, 177–8. For further references see Louis Ginzberg, *The Legends of the Jews* (Philadelphia, Jewish Publication Society of America, 1968), vol. 5, p. 199, nn. 79, 80; p. 276, nn. 38, 39.
161 B. Heller, 'Namrūd', EIS, p. 438.
162 R. 4, pp. 291–2.
163 For example the mass infanticide by the giant Nimrod in an attempt to kill the infant Abraham (R. 2, pp. 350, 352), and the claim by the gnat (*al-baqq*) that it was the smallest member of the insect world (i.e. itself) which was responsible for the death of Nimrod – an obvious reference to an alternative version of his death in which he is tormented for 400 years by a gnat, which enters his brain via his nostrils, before he finally dies (R. 2, pp. 256–7).
164 R. 1, p. 376, R. 2, pp. 231, 266, 280; see n. 157 of these notes for Qur'ānic references; *Genesis Rabbah* XXXVIII:13 on Genesis 11:28: *Midrash Rabbah: Genesis 1* ed. by H. Freedman and M. Simon, (London, Soncino Press, 1961).
165 R. 2, p. 266.
166 R. 1, pp. 376–7; Q. XXI:69. The Ikhwān claim that Nimrod was instructed in the use of the mangonel (*al-minjanīq* or *al-manjanīq*) by the jinn (R. 2, p. 231). The word 'mangonel' does not occur in the Qur'ānic references to the story of Abraham and Nimrod but we find it used, for example, in the account of the ninth-century historian al-Ya'qūbī (*Ta'rīkh al- Ya'qūbī*, (Beirut, Dār Ṣādir, 1960), vol. 1, p. 24). Its use as a tool of execution is recorded elsewhere as well: for example the great medieval traveller Ibn Baṭṭūṭa (1304–1368/9 or 1377) notes that Sultan Muḥammad ibn Tughluq of Delhi ordered that a cripple, left behind in Delhi after the Sultan had ordered the city's evacuation, should be flung to his death from one (*Riḥla* (Beirut, Dār Ṣādir, 1964), p. 479).
167 al-Ṭabarī, *Ta'wīl*, pt 17, p. 45; Ibn al-Athīr, *al-Kāmil fī 'l-Ta'rīkh* (Beirut, Dār Ṣādir, 1965), vol. 1, p. 99.
168 *Pesaḥim* 118a: *Hebrew–English Edition of the Babylonian Talmud*, trans. by H. Freedman and ed. by I. Epstein (London, Soncino Press, 1967); see Daniel 3:24.
169 R. 4, pp. 292–3; Genesis 30:25–43.
170 R. 4, pp. 293–4; 1 Samuel 10, 15, 28, 31.
171 R. 1, pp. 300–1; see above p. 14.
172 Hippocrates (*Buqrāṭ*): R. 2, p. 145; J. 1, p. 430. Galen (*Jālīnūs*): R. 3, p. 330, R. 4, pp. 181, 414, 415, 419, 422–3. For the humours see Galen, *On the Natural Faculties* 11:VIII–IX, trans. by A. J. Brock, *Loeb Classical Library* (London, W. Heinemann/ New York, G. P. Putman's Sons, 1928); see also *Kitāb Buqrāṭ fī 'l-Akhlāṭ (Hippocrates: On Humours) and Kitāb al-Ghidhā' li-Buqrāṭ (Hippocrates: On Nutriment)*, ed. and trans, by J. N. Mattock, *Arabic Technical & Scientific Texts 6* (Cambridge, Heffer, 1971).
173 R. 4, p. 16; see also ibid., pp. 14–15; R. 2, p. 141; R. 3, p. 12.
174 'A. 'Awā, op. cit., p. 306.
175 S. Lane-Poole, op. cit., p. 207.
176 R. 1, pp. 308–10. S. M. Stern rightly saw the Zoroastrian as a prototype of the Brethren. He believed that this story originated in some Zoroastrian polemical writings and noted that Abū Ḥayyān al-Tawḥīdī copied out the story from the *Rasā'il*

into one of his works (S. M. Stern, 'The Authorship', p. 370; al-Tawḥīdī, *al-Imtā' wa 'l-Mu'ānasa*, pt 2, pp. 157–60). Indeed, the tale seem to have been a popular one and was reproduced, for example, in the pseudo-Aristotelian *Sirr al-Asrār* (S. M. Stern, 'Additional Notes to the Article: "The Authorship of the Epistles of the Ikhwān aṣ-Ṣafā" ', *Islamic Culture* 21 (1947), p. 403; *Fontes Graecae Doctrinarum Politicarum Islamicarum*, ed. by A. Badawī (Cairo, Dār al-Kutub al-Miṣriyya, 1954), pt 1, pp. 140–42).

CHAPTER FIVE

1 R. 4, p. 165.
2 Yves Marquet, 'Ikhwān al-Ṣafā'', p. 1071.
3 R. 4, p. 18; see ibid., pp. 269–70, R. 3, pp. 315–20; see Q. XVIII, which is entitled *The Sūra of the Cave*. For a full survey of the legend and cult of the Seven Sleepers of Ephesus, from which the Ikhwān's metaphor ultimately derives, see R. Paret, 'Aṣḥāb al-Kahf', EI2, vol. 1, p. 691, and L. Massignon, *Le Culte Liturgique et Populaire des VII Dormants Martyrs d'Ephèse (Ahl al-Kahf)* in *Opera Minora de Louis Massignon*, ed. by Y. Moubarac (Beirut, Dār al-Ma'ārif, 1963), vol. 3, pp. 119–80.
4 R. 4, p. 166.
5 ibid., p. 269.
6 R. 1, p. 328.
7 Yves Marquet, 'Révélation et Vision Véridique', p. 41.
8 T. J. de Boer, op. cit., p. 85.
9 R. 4, pp. 245–9.
10 ibid.; R. 4, pp. 290–1 and R. 1, p. 346. It is interesting that the traditional chronology of *sūra* titles is preserved in all these citations.
11 A. J. Arberry translates the title as *The Battlements*; see R. Paret, 'al-A'rāf', EI2, vol. 1, pp. 603–4.
12 For example R. 3, pp. 65, 310, 314, 449; R. 4, pp. 246, 290.
13 Q. VII:52, Q. X:3, Q.XIII:2, Q. XXV:60, Q. XXXII:3, Q. LVII:4; see Q. XX:4.
14 R. 3, pp. 344–45.
15 Q. II:272; R. 3, p. 344; see R. 1, p. 348.
16 R. 3, pp. 378–83; see M. S. Seale's article entitled 'The Mysterious Letters of the Qur'an' in his *Qur'an and Bible* (London, Croom Helm, 1978), pp. 29–46.
17 Q. XIII:18; R. 4, pp. 76–7; see also R. 3, pp. 299–300.
18 Q. XIV:29.
19 See his *Anwār al-Tanzīl* (Cairo, al-Ḥalabī, 1939), vol. 1, pp. 427–8.
20 Q. XCV:4; R. 2, pp. 210–11.
21 Singular *sharaf*. The Ikhwān explain: 'The *sharaf* is the most powerful place for the stars in the Sphere . . . [e.g.] the *sharaf* of the sun is in Aries which is the house of Mars' (R. 1, p. 120); see R. Dozy, *Supplément aux Dictionnaires Arabes*, 3rd edn, (Leiden, E. J. Brill/Paris, G. P. Maisonneuve et Larose, 1967), vol. 1, p. 749.
22 The pivots (*awtād*) were the four most powerful Solar Houses or Signs of the Zodiac (R. Dozy, op. cit., vol. 2, p. 778).
23 *La Philosophie des Ikhwān al-Ṣafā'*, pp. 214, 416.
24 Q. XXVII:60. A few variations occur in the quotation of this verse: these include the intercalation in two places (R. 2, pp. 378, 417) of the words *wa kafā* ('That's enough!') after 'Praise belongs to God'. It has been suggested to me by Dr G. H. A. Juynboll that this may be a piece of *tafsīr* which has crept into the quotation. In the very first epistle of the *Rasā'il* the last part of the verse is omitted (R. 1, p. 48).
25 Q. VI:96, Q. XXXVI:38, Q. XLI:11.
26 R. 1, p. 165, R. 4, pp. 274, 270; see also J. 1, pp. 60, 155.

27 R. 2, pp. 206–7.
28 A. Guillaume, 'The Influence of Judaism on Islam' in *The Legacy of Israel*, ed. by E. R. Bevan and C. Singer (Oxford, Clarendon Press, 1944), p. 143.
29 This pride of Iblīs is several times cited beside the greed of Adam and the envy of Cain: R. 1, p. 351, R. 3, p. 458, R. 4, p. 44.
30 For example see Q. XXXVIII:71–6 in R. 4, p. 248; Q. II:32 in R. 4, p. 245; Q. VII:10 in R. 4, p. 246; Q. XV:31, Q. XVII:63–6, and Q. XVIII:48 in R. 4, p. 247. (Qur'ānic citations in the *Rasā'il*, here and elsewhere, are not always of the *complete* verse(s) mentioned in these notes.) See also R. 2, pp. 229–30 where Iblīs is called '*Azāzīl*, a non-Qur'ānic name deriving from the Levitical 'Azāzēl; see Leviticus 16:8, 10, 26 and G. Vajda, ''Azāzīl', EI2, vol. 1, p. 811; see also R. 4, p. 101.
31 For example R. 1, pp. 143, 306; R. 2, pp. 136, 181, 283, 353; R. 3, pp. 18, 141, 414, 475; J. 1, p. 148. Adam is also described as 'the Earth-formed Father of Man (*Abū 'l-Bashar al-Turābī*)' in R. 3, p. 427, see also p. 512.
32 R. 4, p. 376.
33 Q. II:28; R. 3, p. 141; J. 1, p. 156.
34 Q. III:52; R. 1, p. 297, R. 3, p. 18; J. 1, p. 63. The Ikhwān seem to prefer this word to the Qur'ānic alternative 'clay (*ṭīn*)' in Q. VII:11 and Q. XVII:63.
35 R. 4, p. 206; Genesis 1:26–7.
36 R. 2, pp. 229, 332.
37 Genesis 1:28; Q. XVI:5–6 (in R. 2, p. 206), Q. XXXVI:71–3.
38 R. 2, p. 229; Q. II:29–31; Genesis 2:19.
39 R. 2, pp. 332, 229, R. 3, p. 112; see also R. 2, pp. 321–2. *Jabal al-Yāqūt* is Adam's Peak in Ceylon. (See Y. Marquet, *La Philosophie des Iḫwān al-Ṣafā'*, pp. 213–14.) This island was famous for its rubies (R. 2, p. 282; see also Ibn Baṭṭūṭa, op. cit., pp. 596, 600) and identified in Muslim tradition as the place where Adam landed after the expulsion from Paradise. See art. 'Sarandīb' in Yāqūt's *Mu'jam al-Buldān* (Beirut, Dār Ṣādir, 1957), vol. 3, p. 216.
40 R. 2, pp. 229–30; compare Q. VII:19–24; see R. 3, pp. 63 (last line)–64 for a mixture of Q. II:36, Q. VII:23–4 and *tafsīr*.
41 R. 3, p. 159.
42 Q. XLVI:34; R. 3, p. 207.
43 See Q. VII:62 in R. 2, p. 355, and Q. XI:47–8 in R. 4, p. 53.
44 For example R. 2, pp. 148, 280, R. 4, p. 330. In the Qur'ān the word *ṭūfān* is used once to describe the flood of Noah (Q. XXIX:13) and once to describe one of the plagues of Egypt (Q. VII:130).
45 Q. XLIV:9; R. 4, p. 18.
46 R. 1, p. 143; J. 1, pp. 538, 539, J. 2, pp. 147, 232, 353, 374.
47 Q. XLIV:9; R. 2, p. 148.
48 For example R. 2, pp. 142, 280, R. 3, p. 46.
49 Q. IV:124.
50 R. 4, p. 126.
51 For example Q. XXII:77, Q. IV:124.
52 For example R. 4, p. 53, R. 1, p. 376.
53 Q. II:121–2; R. 2, pp. 128–9; compare The Book of Jubilees 22:24 in *The Apocrypha and Pseudepigrapha of the Old Testament in English*, ed. by R. H. Charles (Oxford, Clarendon Press, 1966), vol. 2, p. 47.
54 R. 4, p. 89; Q. XXXVII:101–2.
55 Q. XXXVII:107.
56 R. 4, p. 271 (reading *kharīfan* rather than *kharūfan*); see al-Ṭabarī, *Ta'wīl*, pt 23, pp. 86–7.
57 Q. II:262; R. 4, p. 426. Compare Genesis 15:8–11.
58 Q. XII:46; R. 3, pp. 46, 65, 305, 496, 497, R. 4, pp. 32, 89.
59 R. 3, p. 496.

60 R. 2, p. 231; see Q. XII:15.
61 R. 4, p. 143; see Q. XII:17–18.
62 Q. XII:102; R. 3, p. 46, R. 4, pp. 32, 58.
63 R. 3, p. 46; see al-Ṭabarī, *Ta'wīl*, pt 13, pp. 73–4.
64 R. 2, pp. 280, 351; J. 2, p. 363.
65 R. 1, p. 372; see R. 1, pp. 241, 383–5, 377, R. 4, p. 117; J. 1, p. 389.
66 Q. II:254, Q. IV:162, Q. XIX:53.
67 R. 2, pp. 351–3; see al-Ya'qūbī, op. cit., vol. 1, p. 33.
68 See Q. XX:74–5 in R. 4, p. 27, and Q. VII:118–19 in R. 4, p. 375.
69 R. 2, p. 283; see Q. II:47–54.
70 R. 4, pp. 26–7; Q. II:51; see Exodus 32:27–8.
71 See H. Schwarzbaum, 'Jewish, Christian, Moslem and Falasha Legends of the Death of Aaron, the High Priest', *Fabula* 5 (1962–3), pp. 185–227.
72 R. 4, pp. 27–8.
73 H. Schwarzbaum, op. cit., pp. 206, 214–15.
74 op. cit., vol. 1, p. 41. For similar stories see al-Ṭabarī, *Ta'rīkh*, (Leiden, E. J. Brill, 1879–81), 1st series, vol. 1, pp. 502–3; Ibn al-Athīr, op. cit., vol. 1, p. 197.
75 See H. Schwarzbaum, op. cit., p. 222; G. Eisenberg/G. Vajda, 'Hārūn B. 'Imrān', EI2, vol. 3, p. 231.
76 R. 3, p. 509; Q. XVIII:59–81. See A. J. Wensinck, 'al-Khaḍir (al-Khiḍr)', EI2, vol. 4, pp. 902–5; H. T. Norris, *Saharan Myth and Saga* (Oxford, Clarendon Press, 1972), pp. 14–20.
77 R. 4, p. 28; compare Numbers 14:33–4, 32:13.
78 R. 1, p. 372.
79 Q. XXXVIII:25.
80 R. 3, p. 497; Q. XXXVIII:16, e.g. Q. II:225.
81 R. 3, p. 496.
82 R. 1, p. 207.
83 R. 3, p. 164; 2 Samuel 11.
84 Q. XXXVIII:23; see R. Paret, 'Dāwūd', EI2, vol. 2, p. 182.
85 R. 2, pp. 128–9.
86 R. 3, p. 150.
87 R. 2, pp. 270, 327; see Q. XXVII:16–18.
88 R. 2, p. 249.
89 ibid., pp. 231, 249–50; Q. XXVII:22–5. See also R. 2, pp. 231–2 for the throne episode (Q. XXVII:38–40) in which a member of the jinn is used to bring the Queen of Sheba's throne to Solomon.
90 See Q. XXXIV:11 in R. 4, p. 248; R. 2, pp. 231, 307, 365, R. 4, p. 375; J. 1, p. 540.
91 See Q. XXXIV:13 in R. 4, p. 248; R. 2, pp. 231, 362, 365.
92 R. 2, p. 232; see al-Ṭabarī, *Ta'wīl*, pt 1, pp. 445–50.
93 R. 4, pp. 57–8, 174–5.
94 R. 3, p. 345.
95 C. Pellat, 'al-Baṣra', EI2, vol. 1, p. 1086; 'A. 'Awā, op. cit., pp. 14–16.
96 For example *Hazār-dāstān* or *Hazār-dastān* (nightingale): R. 2, pp. 249, 255, 317; *Shalgham* (turnip): R. 2, p. 162; and the days of the week from Sunday to Thursday: R. 3, p. 207.
97 R. 1, pp. 139, 209, 235.
98 R. 3, pp. 495, 496; see *'Ahd Ardashīr*, ed. by Iḥsān 'Abbās (Beirut, Dār Ṣādir, 1967), pp. 53, 97; al-Mas'ūdī, *Les Prairies d'Or* [*Murūj al-Dhahab*], texte et traduction par C. Barbier de Meynard and P. de Courteille, (Paris, Société Asiatique, 1914), vol. 2, p. 162; R. C. Zaehner, *The Dawn and Twilight of Zoroastrianism* (London, Weidenfeld & Nicolson, 1961), p. 284; see also R. 1, p. 292, R. 2, p. 280.
99 R. 4, p. 148; see also R. 2, p. 460, R. 3, pp. 82–3, 173–6, 315–19, R. 4, pp. 20–2, 148–51, 162–4, 315–27.

100 'The Authorship', p. 370.
101 D. M. Lang, 'Bilawhar wa-Yūdāsaf', EI2, vol. 1, pp. 1215–17; *Kitāb Bilawhar wa Būdhāsf*, ed. by Daniel Gimaret (Beirut, Dār al-Mashriq, 1972); Ibn Bābūya, *Kitāb Ikmāl al-Dīn* (al-Najaf, al-Ḥaydariyya, 1970), pp. 536–600.
102 R. 2, p. 282.
103 R. 4, pp. 58, 175; see *Kitāb Bilawhar*, ed. Gimaret, p. 59; Ibn Bābūya, op. cit., p. 565.
104 R. 4, p. 152. This framework technique came from India via the Iranians. See J. Rypka, *History of Iranian Literature* (Dordrecht, Reidel, 1968), p. 663.
105 R. 4, p. 149.
106 ibid., pp. 152–7; *Kitāb Bilawhar*, ed. Gimaret, pp. 58–9; Ibn Bābūya, op. cit., pp. 564–5.
107 R. 4, pp. 162–4; see Ibn Bābūya, op. cit., p. 592.
108 R. 4, pp. 148–51; *Kitāb Bilawhar*, ed. Gimaret, pp. 32–4; Ibn Bābūya, op. cit., pp. 548–9.
109 R. 4, pp. 14–16; compare *Kitāb Bilawhar*, ed. Gimaret, pp. 157–8, where the people of the city are mad.
110 op. cit., p. 1216.
111 R. 2, pp. 203–377.
112 See above pp. 50, 71.
113 R. 2, p. 377.
114 *Kitāb al-Ḥayawān* (Cairo, al-Ḥalabī, 1966), vol. 5, pp. 542–5.
115 See F. Gabrieli, 'Ibn al-Muḳaffaʿ', EI2, vol. 3, pp. 883–5.
116 R. 2, p. 244; see also pp. 248, 330.
117 See above pp. 4–5. The story of the ring-dove corresponds to the second book of the *Panchatantra* called *The Winning of Friends*; see *The Panchatantra Reconstructed*, text, critical apparatus, introduction and translation by Franklin Edgerton (New York, Kraus, 1967 (Reprint of New Haven, American Oriental Society, 1924 edition)), vol. 1, pp. 181–271, vol. 2, pp. 329–57. See also W. N. Brown, 'A Comparative Translation of the Arabic Kalīla wa-Dimna, Chapter VI', *Journal of the American Oriental Society* 42 (1922), pp. 215–50.
118 R. 2, p. 474; *Kalīla wa Dimna*, pp. 186–209; *The Panchatantra Reconstructed*, vol. 1, pp. 272–370, vol. 2, pp. 358–92.
119 R. 1, p. 391; *Kalīla wa Dimna*, pp. 189–95; *The Panchatantra Reconstructed*, vol. 1, pp. 288–311, vol. 2, pp. 364–72.
120 R. 3, pp. 170–1.
121 ibid., pp. 167–8. Despite consulting a number of scholars of Sanskrit and Pali I have been unable to find an Indian source for these two tales. Professor S. Diwald has suggested to me that they may be of Persian rather than Indian origin.

CHAPTER SIX

1 See above, p. 4.
2 R. 3, p. 401.
3 R. 2, p. 367, R. 3, p. 161.
4 R. 2, p. 367.
5 *Risāla* 42: *On Doctrines and Religions*: R. 3, pp. 401–538.
6 R. 3, pp. 404, 413.
7 ibid., p. 416.
8 ibid., p. 448.
9 ibid., p. 461.
10 ibid., p. 493.
11 ibid., pp. 514, 517.

12 ibid., p. 518.
13 ibid., p. 488.
14 ibid., pp. 490–1.
15 for example ibid., p. 498.
16 R. 2, p. 367; see also R. 3, p. 161, R. 4, pp. 68, 121.
17 See W. Madelung, 'Ismā'īliyya', EI2, vol. 4, pp. 198–206, for a good introduction to Ismā'īlī doctrine and history.
18 A. A. A. Fyzee, 'The Ismā'īlīs' in *Religion in the Middle East*, ed. by A. J. Arberry *et al.*, vol. 2, p. 324.
19 Yves Marquet, 'Ikhwān al-Ṣafā'', p. 1071.
20 Hossein Nasr, *Cosmological Doctrines*, p. 27.
21 ibid., pp. 25–36.
22 ibid., p. 36.
23 S. M. Stern, 'New Information about the Authors of the "Epistles of the Sincere Brethren" ', *Islamic Studies*, vol. 3, no. 4 (1964), p. 417.
24 ibid., p. 421.
25 B. Lewis, *The Origins of Ismā'īlism* (Cambridge, Heffer, 1940; this important work was reprinted by AMS Press, New York, in 1975), p. 17.
26 ibid., p. 44.
27 'Ikhwān aṣ-Ṣafā and their Rasā'il', pp. 33, 40, 43.
28 'A. 'Awā, op. cit., pp. 35–45.
29 Seyyed Hossein Nasr, 'Philosophy and Cosmology' in *The Cambridge History of Iran. Volume 4: The Period from the Arab Invasion to the Saljuqs*, ed. by R. N. Frye (Cambridge, Cambridge University Press, 1975), p. 428.
30 'Scientific Elements in Ismā'īlī Thought: the Epistles of the Brethren of Purity (*Ikhwān al-Ṣafā'*)' in *Ismā'īlī Contributions to Islamic Culture*, ed. by Seyyed Hossein Nasr (Teheran, Imperial Iranian Academy of Philosophy, 1977), p. 123.
31 *The Ismā'īlīs*, p. 329.
32 al-Shahrastānī, *al-Milal wa 'l-Niḥal*, ed. by Muḥammad Sayyid Kīlānī (Cairo, al-Ḥalabī, 1967), vol. 1, p. 24. (The author's name is also spelled al-Shahristānī.)
33 al-Nu'mān b. Muḥammad, *Da'ā'im al-Islām*, ed. by A. A. A. Fyzee (Cairo, Dār al-Ma'ārif, 1963), vol. 1, p. 45.
34 Q. IV:62.
35 *Da'ā'im*, vol. 1, p. 25.
36 ibid., pp. 39–40.
37 A. A. A. Fyzee, *Outlines of Muhammadan Law* (London, Oxford University Press, 1964), p. 42.
38 For example al-Nu'mān b. Muḥammad, *Ikhtilāf Uṣūl al-Madhāhib*, ed. by S. T. Lokhandwalla (Simla, Indian Institute of Advanced Study, 1972), p. 230.
39 See al-Māwardī, *al-Aḥkām al-Sulṭāniyya* (Cairo, al-Ḥalabī, 1973), pp. 17–20.
40 Ḥusain F. al-Hamdānī, 'Rasā'il Ikhwān aṣ-Ṣafā in the literature of the Ismā'īlī Ṭaiyibī Da'wat', *Der Islam* 20 (1932), pp. 286–7.
41 R. 4, p. 18.
42 'A. 'Awā, op. cit., pp. 42–3; I. R. al-Fārūqī, op. cit., *Muslim World* 51 (January 1961), p. 22. I have followed al-Fārūqī here and applied the epithet *al-Akbar* (Greatest or Supreme) to the word 'Master' in my translation of *Ṣāḥib al-Nāmūs al-Akbar*. 'Awā, however, believes that *al-Akbar* describes 'the Law'.
43 Yves Marquet, 'La Place du Travail dans la Hiérarchie Ismā'īlienne d'après *L'Encyclopédie des Frères de la Pureté*', *Arabica*, vol. 8, no. 3 (1961), p. 226.
44 R. 3, p. 493.
45 ibid., p. 494.
46 op. cit., p. 286.
47 As in the passage in R. 3, p. 493, cited above; 'A. 'Awā, op. cit., p. 41.
48 R. 4, 376; see Q. II:28.

49 R. 2, p. 300.
50 R. 4, p. 377.
51 ibid., p. 380.
52 ibid., p. 148.
53 R. 3, pp. 488–9.
54 Yves Marquet, 'Imamat', p. 49.
55 Marquet translates both *wāḍi' al-sharī'a* and the following *wāḍi' al-nāmūs* as 'law-giver' (*législateur*) and elsewhere identifies five principal ones: Noah, Abraham, Moses, Jesus and Muḥammad ('Imamat', p. 49; idem, *La Philosophie des Iḫwān al-Ṣafā'*, p. 321; R. 3, p. 380). Henry Corbin translates the similar phrase *ṣāḥib al-sharī'a* (R. 4, p. 270) as 'founder' or 'establisher of the law' (*l'instaurateur de la loi*), ('Rituel Sabéen et Exégèse Ismaélienne du Rituel', *Eranos Jahrbuch* 19 (1950), p. 216).
56 R. 4, p. 137.
57 'Imamat', pp. 49, 63.
58 R. 4, p. 380; see 'A. 'Awā, op. cit., p. 44.
59 R. 3, p. 483; Yves Marquet, 'Imamat', p. 59.
60 R. 4, p. 17; Yves Marquet, 'Imamat', p. 59.
61 R. 4, pp. 33, 75, 269; Yves Marquet, 'Imamat', p. 59.
62 R., 2, p. 290.
63 For example Yves Marquet, 'Imamat', pp. 55–8.
64 For example R. 1, p. 377, R. 4, pp. 17, 195; see Ḥ. F. Hamdānī, op. cit., pp. 285–6. For the translation of the title *Amīr al-Mu'minīn*, and its development in early Islamic history, see M. A. Shaban, *Islamic History: A.D. 600–750 (A.H. 132): a New Interpretation* (Cambridge, Cambridge University Press, 1971), pp. 56–7, 60–2, 79, 111, 116–17, 167, 179–80, 187–8.
65 'A. 'Awā, op. cit., p. 40.
66 'Imamat', pp. 55–8.
67 R. 4, p. 16.
68 ibid., p. 73.
69 ibid., pp. 74–5.
70 R. 1, p. 346.
71 'A. 'Awā, op. cit., p. 42.
72 op. cit., p. 41.
73 R. 4, pp. 129–30; 'Imamat', pp. 49, 63.
74 R. 4, pp. 130–1.
75 R. 3, pp. 494–5.
76 ibid., p. 495; see 'A. 'Awā, op. cit., p. 41.
77 For example R. 3, p. 306, R. 4, pp. 25, 109; see Plato, *Phaedo*, 64B–66E.
78 See above pp. 67–8.
79 R. 2, p. 290.
80 For example R. 4, pp. 18, 269.
81 For example R. 4, pp. 379, 381; J. 1, pp. 112, 115, 126.
82 R. 4, p. 270.
83 al-Nu'mān b. Muḥammad, *Da'ā'im al-Islām*, ed. by A. A. A. Fyzee (Cairo, Dār al-Ma'ārif, 1960), vol. 2, p. 130.
84 R. 4, p. 148; see R. 3, p. 523; see 'A. 'Awā, op. cit., pp. 44, 249; Yves Marquet, 'Ikhwān al-Ṣafā' ', p. 1071; idem, 'Imamat', pp. 62, 69. Casanova regarded the use of the term *ẓāhir* in the quotation as a play on words of the Fāṭimid Caliph al-Ẓāhir who reigned from 1021–36 ('Une Date Astronomique', pp. 16–17).
85 Yves Marquet, 'Imamat', p. 80.
86 R. 4, pp. 125–6.
87 See A. L. Tibawi, 'Ikhwān aṣ-Ṣafā and their Rasā'il', p. 34.
88 R. 4, p. 126.

89 ibid., p. 44.
90 ibid., pp. 54–5.
91 ibid., p. 48.
92 op. cit., pp. 15–16; see Muhammad Qamaruddin Khan, 'al-Māwardi' in *A History of Muslim Philosophy*, ed. by M. M. Sharif (Wiesbaden, Otto Harrassowitz, 1963), vol. 1, pp. 726–7.
93 R. 4, p. 127.
94 Yves Marquet, *La Philosophie des Iḫwān al-Ṣafā'*, p. 585.

CONCLUSION

1 For example R. 2, p. 286.
2 See above p. 78; see Abbas Hamdani, 'An Early Fāṭimid Source on the Time and Authorship of the *Rasā'il Iḫwān al-Ṣafā'*', *Arabica*, vol. 26, no. 1 (1979), p. 73.
3 Hossein Nasr, *Cosmological Doctrines*, pp. 31, 33.
4 See ibid., pp. 4–5, 104.
5 A. L. Tibawi, 'Ikhwān aṣ-Ṣafā and their Rasā'il', p. 44.
6 R. 4, p. 165.
7 See above, p. 41; see R. 3, p. 511.
8 See above, p. 118 n. 53.
9 R. 4, p. 18.

Bibliography

(This is not a comprehensive bibliography of sources for the study of the Ikhwān al-Ṣafā' but is restricted to those sources cited in my footnotes and preface.)

ARABIC SOURCES

Ardashīr 1, *'Ahd Ardashīr*, ed. by Iḥsān 'Abbās (Beirut, Dār Ṣādir, 1967).

Badawī, 'Abd al-Raḥmān (ed.), *Fontes Graecae Doctrinarum Politicarum Islamicarum*, pt 1 (Cairo, Dār al-Kutub al-Miṣriyya, 1954).

Badawī, 'Abd al-Raḥmān (ed.), *Manṭiq Arisṭū*, pt 1 (Cairo, Dār al-Kutub al-Miṣriyya, 1948).

al-Bayḍāwī, Nāṣir al-Dīn 'Abd Allāh, *Anwār al-Tanzīl*, vol 1 (Cairo, al-Ḥalabī, 1939).

al-Bukhārī, Muḥammad b. Ismā'īl, *Ṣaḥīḥ*, pt 4 (Cairo, al-Ḥalabī, 1926).

Buqrāt (Hippocrates), *Kitāb Buqrāṭ fī'l-Akhlāt (Hippocrates: On Humours) and Kitāb al-Ghidhā' li-Buqrāṭ (Hippocrates: On Nutriment)*, ed. and trans. by J. N. Mattock. *Arabic Technical & Scientific Texts 6* (Cambridge, Heffer, 1971).

Gimaret, Daniel (ed.), *Kitāb Bilawhar wa Būdhāsf* (Beirut, Dār al-Mashriq, 1972).

al-Ḥallāj, al-Ḥusayn b. Manṣūr, *Akhbār al-Ḥallāj*, publié, annoté et traduit par L. Massignon et P. Kraus (Paris, Editions–Larose, 1936).

Ibn al-Athīr, 'Izz al-Dīn, *al-Kāmil fī 'l-Ta'rīkh*, vol. 1 (Beirut, Dār Ṣādir, 1965).

Ibn Bābūya (Ibn Bābawayhi), Muḥammad b. 'Alī, *Kitāb Ikmāl al-Dīn* (al-Najaf, al-Ḥaydariyya, 1970).

Ibn Baṭṭūṭa, Muḥammad b. 'Abd Allāh, *Riḥla* (Beirut, Dār Ṣādir, 1964).

Ibn Ḥanbal, Aḥmad, *Musnad*, vol. 2 (Beirut, Dār Ṣādir, n.d.).

Ibn Hishām, 'Abd al-Malik/Ibn Isḥāq, Muḥammad, *The Life of Muhammad. A Translation of Isḥāq's Sīrat Rasūl Allāh*, by A. Guillaume (O.U.P. Pakistan Branch, 1955).

Ibn Hishām, 'Abd al-Malik/Ibn Isḥāq, Muḥammad, *al-Sīrat al-Nabawiyya*, vol. 1, ed. by M. Saqqā *et al.* (Cairo, al-Ḥalabī, 1955).

Ibn Māja, Muḥammad b. Yazīd, *Sunan*, vol. 2 (Cairo, Dār Iḥyā' al-Kutub al-'Arabiyya, 1954).

Ibn al-Muqaffa', 'Abd Allāh, *Āthār Ibn al-Muqaffa'* (Beirut, Dār Maktabat al-Ḥayāt, 1966).

Ikhwān al-Ṣafā', *Ikhwanu-Ṣ-Ṣafā; or, Brothers of Purity*, trans. from the Urdu by J. Platts (London, W. H. Allen, 1875).

Ikhwān al-Ṣafā', *Rasā'il Ikhwān al-Ṣafā'*, 4 vols, ed. by Khayr al-Dīn Zarkalī (Cairo, 'Arabiyya Press, 1928).

Ikhwān al-Ṣafā', *Rasā'il Ikhwān al-Ṣafā'*, 4 vols, (Beirut, Dār Ṣādir, 1957).

Ikhwān al-Ṣafā', *al-Risālat al-Jāmi'a*, 2 vols, ed. by J. Salībā (Damascus, al-Taraqqī Press, 1949).

al-Jāḥiẓ, 'Amr b. Baḥr, *Kitāb al-Ḥayawān*, vol. 5 (Cairo, al-Ḥalabī, 1966).

al-Jāḥiẓ, 'Amr b. Baḥr, *Thalāth Rasā'il*, ed. by J. Finkel, (Cairo, Salafiyya Press, 1926).

al-Khawārizmī, Muḥammad b. Aḥmad, *Mafātīḥ al-'Ulūm*, ed. by G. Van Vloten (Leiden, E. J. Brill, 1895).

al-Kindī, Ya'qūb b. Isḥāq, *Rasā'il al-Kindī al-Falsafiyya*, vol. 1, ed. by M. A. Abū Rīdah (Cairo, Dār al-Fikr al-'Arabī, 1950).

al-Maqrīzī, Aḥmad b. 'Alī, *Kitāb al-Mawā'iz wa 'l-I'tibār bi-Dhikr al-Khiṭaṭ wa 'l-Āthār*, vol. 1 (Baghdad, al-Muthannā, n.d.).

al-Mas'ūdī, 'Alī b. al-Ḥusayn, *Les Prairies d'Or* [*Murūj al-Dhahab*], vol. 2, texte et traduction par C. Barbier de Meynard et P. de Courteille (Paris, Société Asiatique, 1914).

al-Māwardī, 'Alī b. Muḥammad, *al-Aḥkām al-Sulṭāniyya* (Cairo, al-Ḥalabī, 1973).

Muslim b. al-Ḥajjāj, *al-Jāmi' al-Ṣaḥīḥ*, pt 8 (Cairo, Dār al-Taḥrīr, 1964).

al-Nadīm, Muḥammad b. Abī Ya'qūb Isḥāq, *The Fihrist of al-Nadīm*, vol. 2, ed. and trans. by Bayard Dodge (New York and London, Columbia University Press, 1970).

al-Nadīm, Muḥammad b. Abī Ya'qūb Isḥāq, *Kitāb al-Fihrist* (Teheran, Teheran University Press, 1971).

al-Nu'mān b. Muḥammad, *Da'ā'im al-Islām*, vol. 1, ed. by A. A. A. Fyzee (Cairo, Dār al-Ma'ārif, 1963); vol. 2, ed. by A. A. A. Fyzee (Cairo, Dār al-Ma'ārif, 1960).

al-Nu'mān b. Muḥammad, *Ikhtilāf Uṣūl al-Madhāhib*, ed. by S. T. Lokhandwalla (Simla, Indian Institute of Advanced Study, 1972).

Qur'ān, The, *The Koran Interpreted*, 2 vols, by A. J. Arberry (London, Allen & Unwin, 1955).

Riḍā, Rashīd, *Fatāwā*, vol. 2 (Beirut, Dār al-Kitāb al-Jadīd, 1970).

al-Shahrastānī, Muḥammad b. 'Abd al-Karīm, *al-Milal wa 'l-Niḥal*, vol. 1, ed. by Muḥammad Sayyid Kīlānī (Cairo, al-Ḥalabī, 1967).

al-Ṭabarī, Abū Ja'far Muḥammad b. Jarīr, *Jāmi' al-Bayān 'an Ta'wīl Āy al-Qur'ān*, 2nd edn, pts 1, 3, 13, 17, 23 (Cairo, al-Ḥalabī, 1954).

al-Ṭabarī, Abū Ja'far Muḥammad b. Jarīr, *Ta'rīkh*, 1st series, vol. 1 (Leiden, E. J. Brill, 1879–81).

Tāmir, 'Ārif, *Ḥaqīqat Ikhwān al-Ṣafā' wa Khullān al-Wafā'* (Beirut, Imprimerie Catholique, 1966).

al-Tawḥīdī, Abū Ḥayyān, *al-Imtā' wa 'l-Mu'ānasa*, pt 2, ed. by Aḥmad Amīn (Beirut, Dār Maktabat al-Ḥayāt, n.d.).

al-Tirmidhī, Abū 'Īsā Muḥammad, *al-Jāmi' al-Ṣaḥīḥ*, vol. 4 (Cairo, al-Ḥalabī, 1962).

al-Ya'qūbī, Aḥmad b. Abī Ya'qūb, *Ta'rīkh al-Ya'qūbī*, vol. 1 (Beirut, Dār Ṣādir, 1960).

Yāqūt b. 'Abd Allāh al-Ḥamawī, *Mu'jam al-Buldān*, vol. 3 (Beirut, Dār Ṣādir, 1957).

OTHER SOURCES

'Abd al-Tafāhum, 'Doctrine', in *Religion in the Middle East*, vol. 2, ed. by A. J. Arberry *et al.* (Cambridge, Cambridge University Press, 1969).

Abramowski, L., and Goodman, A. E. (eds. and trans.), *A Nestorian Collection of Christological Texts: Cambridge University Library MS. Oriental 1319*, 2 vols (Cambridge, Cambridge University Press, 1972).

Allouche, I. S., 'Un Traité de Polémique Christiano-Musulmane au IXe Siècle', *Hesperis* 26 (1939), pp. 123–55.

Aristotle, *Aristotle's Physics: Books I and II*, trans. by W. Charlton, *Clarendon Aristotle Series* (Oxford, Clarendon Press, 1970).

Aristotle, *Aristotle's Posterior Analytics*, trans. by J. Barnes, *Clarendon Aristotle Series* (Oxford, Clarendon Press, 1975).

Aristotle, *Aristotelis Fragmenta Selecta*, ed. by W. D. Ross (Oxford, Clarendon Press, 1955).

Aristotle, *Generation of Animals*, trans. by A. L. Peck, *Loeb Classical Library* (London, W. Heinemann/Cambridge, Mass., Harvard University Press, 1953).

Aristotle, *The Metaphysics Books I–IX*, trans. by H. Tredennick, *Loeb Classical Library* (London, W. Heinemann/Cambridge, Mass., Harvard University Press, 1968).

Aristotle, *On the Heavens*, trans. by W. K. C. Guthrie, *Loeb Classical Library* (London, W. Heinemann/Cambridge, Mass., Harvard University Press, 1945).

Aristotle, *The Organon 1: The Categories* [*and*] *On Interpretation*, trans. by Harold P. Cooke; and *Prior Analytics*, trans. by Hugh Tredennick, *Loeb Classical Library* (London, W. Heinemann/Cambridge, Mass., Harvard University Press, 1949).

Aristotle, *The Physics*, trans. by P. H. Wicksteed and F. M. Cornford, *Loeb Classical Library* (London, W. Heinemann/Cambridge, Mass., Harvard University Press, 1957).

Aristotle, *Posterior Analytics*, trans. by Hugh Tredennick, and *Topica*, trans. by E. S. Forster, *Loeb Classical Library* (London, W. Heinemann/Cambridge, Mass., Harvard University Press, 1960).

Aristotle, *Select Fragments*, ed. by W. D. Ross, *The Works of Aristotle Translated into English: vol. 12* (Oxford, Clarendon Press, 1952).

Armstrong, A. H., 'Plotinus' in *The Cambridge History of Later Greek and Early Medieval Philosophy*, ed. by A. H. Armstrong (Cambridge, Cambridge University Press, 1967).

Arnaldez, R., 'Ḥaraka wa Sukūn', EI2, vol. 3, pp. 169–72.

Atiyeh, George N., *al-Kindī: the Philosopher of the Arabs* (Rawalpindi, Islamic Research Institute, 1966).

'Awā, 'A., *L'Esprit Critique des 'Frères de la Pureté: Encyclopédistes arabes du IVe/Xe siècle* (Beirut, Imprimerie Catholique, 1948).

Bausani, Alessandro, *L'Enciclopedia dei Fratelli della Purità* (Naples, Istituto Universitario Orientale, 1978).

Bausani, Alessandro, 'Scientific Elements in Ismā'īlī Thought: the Epistles of the Brethren of Purity (*Ikhwān al-Ṣafā'*)' in *Ismā'īlī Contributions to Islamic*

Culture, ed. by Seyyed Hossein Nasr (Teheran, Imperial Iranian Academy of Philosophy, 1977), pp. 123–40.

Brockelmann, C., *Geschichte der arabischen Litteratur*, vol. 1 (Weimar, E. Felber, 1898).

Brockelmann, C., *Geschichte der arabischen Litteratur*, vol. 1 (Leiden, E. J. Brill, 1943).

Brockelmann, C., *Erster Supplementband* (Leiden, E. J. Brill, 1937).

Brown, W. N., 'A Comparative Translation of the Arabic Kalīla wa-Dimna, Chapter VI', *Journal of the American Oriental Society* 42 (1922), pp. 215–50.

Carra de Vaux, B., 'al-Ṣābi'a', EIS, pp. 477–78.

Carra de Vaux, B., and Anawati, G. C., 'Indjīl', EI2, vol. 3, pp. 1205–8.

Casanova, P., 'Une Date Astronomique dans les Épîtres des Ikhwān aṣ Ṣafā', *Journal Asiatique* 5 (1915), pp. 5–17.

Charles, R. H. (ed.), *The Apocrypha and Pseudepigrapha of the Old Testament in English*, vol. 2 (Oxford, Clarendon Press, 1966).

Corbin, Henry, 'Rituel Sabéen et Exégèse Ismaélienne du Rituel', *Eranos Jahrbuch* 19 (1950), pp. 181–246.

Cranfield, C. E. B., *The Gospel According to Saint Mark: an Introduction and Commentary* (Cambridge, Cambridge University Press, 1959).

Daniel, N., *Islam and the West* (Edinburgh, Edinburgh University Press, 1966).

De Boer, T. J., *The History of Philosophy in Islam* (London, Luzac & Co., 1970).

Diels, H., and Kranz, W. (eds), *Die Fragmente der Vorsokratiker*, vol. 1 (Berlin, Weidmann, 1951).

Diogenes Laertius, *Lives of Eminent Philosophers*, vol. 2, trans. by R. D. Hicks, *Loeb Classical Library* (London, W. Heinemann/New York, G. P. Putman's Sons, 1925).

Diwald, Susanne, *Arabische Philosophie und Wissenschaft in der Enzyklopädie Kitāb Iḫwān aṣ-ṣafā' (III): Die Lehre von Seele und Intellekt*, (Wiesbaden, Otto Harrassowitz, 1975).

Dozy, R., *Supplément aux Dictionnaires Arabes*, 3rd edn, 2 vols (Leiden, E. J. Brill/Paris, G. P. Maisonneuve et Larose, 1967).

Edgerton, Franklin (ed. and trans.), *The Panchatantra Reconstructed*, 2 vols, text, critical apparatus, introduction and translation by Franklin Edgerton (New York, Kraus, 1967 (Reprint of New Haven, American Oriental Society, 1924 edn)).

Eisenberg, G., and Vajda, G., 'Hārūn B. 'Imrān', EI2, vol. 3, pp. 231–2.

Encyclopaedia of Islam, New edition, 4 vols completed, vol. 5 continuing; ed. by H. A. R. Gibb *et al.* (Leiden, E. J. Brill/ London, Luzac & Co., 1960–).

Fabre d'Olivet, A., *The Golden Verses of Pythagoras*, trans. by N. L. Redfield (Wellingborough, Thorsons, 1975).

Fackenheim, Emil L., 'The Conception of Substance in the Philosophy of the Ikhwan as-Safa' (*Brethren of Purity*)', *Medieval Studies* (Toronto) 5 (1943), pp. 115–22.

Fakhry, M., *A History of Islamic Philosophy* (New York and London, Columbia University Press, 1970).

Flügel, G., 'Über Inhalt und Verfasser der arabischen Encyclopädie *Rasā'il Ikhwān al-Ṣafā wa Khullān al-Wafā* d.i. die Abhandlungen der aufrichtigen Brüder und treuen Freunde', *Zeitschrift der Deutschen morgenländischen Gesellschaft* 13 (1859), pp. 1–43.

al-Fārūqī, I. R., 'On the Ethics of the Brethren of Purity', *Muslim World* 50 (April 1960), pp. 109–21; 50 (October 1960), pp. 252–8; 51 (January 1961), pp. 18–24.

Friedlander, Gerald (ed. and trans.), *Pirḳê De Rabbi Eliezer*, ed. and trans. by Gerald Friedlander (New York, Hermon Press, 1970 (Reprint of London, Kegan Paul, 1916 edn)).

Fyzee, A. A. A., 'The Ismā'īlīs' in *Religion in the Middle East*, vol. 2, ed. by A. J. Arberry *et al.* (Cambridge, Cambridge University Press, 1969).

Fyzee, A. A. A., *Outlines of Muhammadan Law* (London, Oxford University Press, 1964).

Gabrieli, F., 'Ibn al-Muḳaffa'', EI2, vol. 3, pp. 883–5.

Galen, *On the Natural Faculties*, trans. by A. J. Brock, *Loeb Classical Library* (London, W. Heinemann/New York, G. P. Putnam's Sons, 1928).

Gardet, L., 'Djanna', EI2, vol. 2, pp. 447–52.

Gibb, H. A. R., *Arabic Literature*, 2nd rev. edn (Oxford, Clarendon Press, 1963).

Giffen, L. A., *Theory of Profane Love among the Arabs: The Development of the Genre* (New York, New York University Press/London, University of London Press, 1971–2).

Ginzberg, Louis, *The Legends of the Jews*, vol. 5 (Philadelphia, Jewish Publication Society of America, 1968).

Goichon, A. M., 'Ḥikma', EI2, vol. 3, pp. 377–8.

Goldziher, Ignaz, 'Abdāl', EI2, vol. 1, pp. 94–5.

Goldziher, Ignaz, *Muslim Studies*, vol. 2, trans. by C. R. Barber and S. M. Stern (London, Allen & Unwin, 1971).

Goldziher, Ignaz, 'Über die Benennung der "Ichwān al-ṣafā" ', *Der Islam* 1 (1910), pp. 22–6.

Goldziher, Ignaz, and Goichon, A. M., 'Dahriyya', EI2, vol. 2, pp. 95–7.

Graham, William A., *Divine Word and Prophetic Word in Early Islam* (The Hague, Mouton, 1977).

Guillaume, A., 'The Influence of Judaism on Islam' in *The Legacy of Israel*, ed. by E. R. Bevan and C. Singer (Oxford, Clarendon Press, 1944).

Guillaume, A., *The Traditions of Islam*, *Khayats Oriental Reprint No. 13* (Beirut, Khayats, 1966).

Guillaumont, A., Puech, H.-Ch., *et al.* (eds and trans.), *The Gospel according to Thomas*, Coptic text estab. and trans. by the eds (Leiden, E. J. Brill/London, Collins, 1959).

Gutas, D., *Greek Wisdom Literature in Arabic Translation: a Study of the Graeco-Arabic Gnomologia* (New Haven, American Oriental Society, 1975).

Hamdani, Abbas, 'Abū Ḥayyān al-Tawḥīdī and the Brethren of Purity', *International Journal of Middle East Studies*, vol. 9, no. 3 (1978), pp. 345–53.

Hamdani, Abbas, 'An Early Fāṭimid Source on the Time and Authorship of the *Rasā'il Iḫwān al-Ṣafā*' ', *Arabica* vol. 26, no. 1 (1979), pp. 62–75.

al-Hamdānī, Ḥusain F., 'Rasā'il Ikhwān aṣ-Ṣafā in the literature of the Ismā'īlī Ṭaiyibī Da'wat', *Der Islam* 20 (1932), pp. 281–300.

Hammond, N. G. L. and Scullard, H. H. (eds), *The Oxford Classical Dictionary*, 2nd edn (Oxford, Clarendon Press, 1970).

Heller, B., 'Namrūd', EIS, pp. 437–8.

Hennecke, E., *New Testament Apocrypha*, vol. 1, ed. by W. Schneemelcher (London, Lutterworth Press, 1963).

Hodgson, M. G. S., 'Bāṭiniyya', EI2, vol. 1, pp. 1098–1100.

Iamblichus, *De Vita Pythagorica Liber*, ed. by L. Deubner and U. Klein (Stuttgart, B. G. Teubner, 1975).

James, M. R. (trans.), *The Apocryphal New Testament* (Oxford, Clarendon Press, 1924, reprinted 1975).

Kelly, J. N. D., *Early Christian Doctrines*, 5th rev. edn (London, A. & C. Black, 1977).

Khan, Muhammad Qamaruddin, 'al-Māwardi' in *A History of Muslim Philosophy*, vol. 1, ed. by M. M. Sharif, (Wiesbaden, Otto Harrassowitz, 1963).

Kirk, G. S., and Raven, J. E., *The Presocratic Philosophers* (Cambridge, Cambridge University Press, 1962).

Kraemer, J., *Das arabische Original des Pseudo-Aristotelischen* Liber de Pomo, in *Studi Orientalistici in onore di Giorgio Levi della Vida*, vol. 1 (Rome, Istituto per L'Oriente, 1956), pp. 484–506.

Lane, E. W., *An Arabic-English Lexicon*, vol. 2, (Beirut, Librairie du Liban, reprinted 1968).

Lane-Poole, S., *Studies in a Mosque, Khayats Oriental Reprint No. 21* (Beirut, Khayats, 1966).

Lang, D. M., 'Bilawhar wa-Yūdāsaf', EI2, vol. 1, pp. 1215–17.

Levonian, L. (trans.), 'The Ikhwān al-Ṣafā' and Christ', *Muslim World* 35 (1945), pp. 27–31.

Lewis, B., *The Origins of Ismā'īlism* (Cambridge, Heffer, 1940 (Reprinted by New York, AMS Press, 1975)).

Macrobius, *Saturnalia*, vol. 1 (Leipzig, B. G. Teubner, 1963).

Macrobius, *The Saturnalia*, trans. by P. V. Davies (New York and London, Columbia University Press, 1969).

Madelung, W., 'Ismā'īliyya', EI2, vol. 4, pp. 198–206.

Margoliouth, D. S., 'The Book of the Apple, ascribed to Aristotle' (ed. in Persian and English), *Journal of the Royal Asiatic Society* (1892), pp. 187–92, 202–52.

Marquet, Yves, 'Coran et Création', *Arabica*, vol. 11 no. 3 (1964), pp. 279–85.

Marquet, Yves, 'Ikhwān al-Ṣafā'', EI2, vol. 3, pp. 1071–6.

Marquet, Yves, 'Imamat, Résurrection et Hiérarchie selon les Ikhwan as-Safā', *Revue des Études Islamiques* 30 (1962), pp. 49–142.

Marquet, Yves, *La Philosophie des Iḫwān al-Ṣafā'*, (Algiers, Société Nationale d'Édition et de Diffusion, 1975).

Marquet, Yves, 'La Place du Travail dans la Hiérarchie Ismā'īlienne d'après *L'Encyclopédie des Frères de la Pureté*', *Arabica*, vol. 8, no. 3 (1961), pp. 225–37.

Marquet, Yves, 'Révélation et Vision Véridique chez les Ikhwān al-Safā'', *Revue des Études Islamiques* 32 (1964), pp. 27–44.

Marquet, Yves, 'Sabéens et Iḫwān al-Ṣafā'', *Studia Islamica* 24 (1966), pp. 35–80.

Massignon, L., *Opera Minora de Louis Massignon*, vol. 3 ed. by Y. Moubarac (Beirut, Dār al-Ma'ārif, 1963).

Massignon, L., 'Sur la date de la composition des "Rasā'il Ikhwān al ṣafa" ', *Der Islam* 4 (1913), p. 324.

Ménard, J. E. (ed. and trans.), *L'Évangile selon Philippe* (Paris, Letouzey & Ané, 1967).

Midrash, *Midrash Rabbah: Genesis 1*, ed. by H. Freedman and M. Simon (London, Soncino Press, 1961).
Midrash, *Midrash Rabbah: Genesis 2*, ed. by H. Freedman and M. Simon (London, Soncino Press, 1961).
Nasr, Seyyed Hossein, *An Introduction to Islamic Cosmological Doctrines* (Cambridge, Mass., Harvard University Press, 1964).
Nasr, Seyyed Hossein, 'Philosophy and Cosmology' in *The Cambridge History of Iran. Volume 4: The Period from the Arab Invasion to the Saljuqs*, ed. R. N. Frye (Cambridge, Cambridge University Press, 1975), pp. 419–41.
Netton, Ian Richard, 'Aristotelianism' in *A Dictionary of Philosophy*, ed. by Antony Flew (London, Pan Books, 1979), pp. 21–3.
Netton, Ian Richard, 'Brotherhood versus Imāmate: Ikhwān al-Ṣafā' and the Ismā'īlīs', *Jerusalem Studies in Arabic and Islam* 2 (1980), pp. 253–62.
Nicholson, R. A., *A Literary History of the Arabs* (Cambridge, Cambridge University Press, 1969).
Nock, A. D., and Festugière, A. J. (eds), *Corpus Hermeticum*, 4 vols (Paris, Société d'Édition 'Les Belles Lettres' 1972).
Norris, H. T., *Saharan Myth and Saga* (Oxford, Clarendon Press, 1972).
Owens, Joseph, *The Doctrine of Being in the Aristotelian 'Metaphysics'* (Toronto, Pontifical Institute of Mediaeval Studies, 1963).
Paret, R., 'al-A'rāf', EI2, vol. 1, pp. 603–4.
Paret, R., 'Aṣḥāb al-Kahf', EI2, vol. 1, p. 691.
Paret, R., 'Dāwūd', EI2, vol. 2, p. 182.
Paret, R., 'Ibrāhīm', EI2, vol. 3, pp. 980–1.
Parrinder, G., *Jesus in the Qur'ān* (London, Faber & Faber, 1965).
Peeters, P., *Évangiles Apocryphes*, vol. 2 (Paris, A. Picard, 1914).
Pellat, C., 'al-Baṣra', EI2, vol. 1, pp. 1085–6.
Peters, F. E., *Aristotle and the Arabs* (New York, New York University Press/ London, University of London Press, 1968).
Peters, F. E., *Aristoteles Arabus* (Leiden, E. J. Brill, 1968).
Philip, J. A., *Pythagoras and Early Pythagoreanism*, (Toronto, University of Toronto Press, 1966).
Phillips, E. D., *Greek Medicine* (London, Thames & Hudson, 1973).
Philoxenus of Mabbug, *Tractatus Tres de Trinitate et Incarnatione*, ed. and trans. by A. Vaschalde, *Corpus Scriptorum Christianorum Orientalium vols. 9, 10, Scriptores Syrii vols. 9, 10* (Reprinted Louvain: Sécretariat du Corpus SCO, 1955, 1961).
Plato, *Euthyphro, Apology, Crito, Phaedo, Phaedrus*, trans. by H. N. Fowler, *Loeb Classical Library* (London, W. Heinemann/Cambridge, Mass., Harvard University Press, 1966).
Plato, *The Republic I Books I–V*, trans. by Paul Shorey, *Loeb Classical Library* (London, W. Heinemann/Cambridge, Mass., Harvard University Press, 1969).
Plessner, M., 'Hermes Trismegistus and Arab Science', *Studia Islamica* 2 (1954), pp. 45–59.
Plessner, M., 'Hirmis', EI2, vol. 3, pp. 463–5.
Plotinus, *Enneads*, 3 vols, (complete to the end of the 3rd *Ennead*), trans. by A. H. Armstrong, *Loeb Classical Library* (London, W. Heinemann/ Cambridge, Mass., Harvard University Press, 1966–7).

Plotinus, *Enneads*, 2nd edn, trans. by S. MacKenna (London, Faber & Faber, 1956).

Plotinus, *Plotini Opera*, 3 vols, ed. by P. Henry and H. R. Schwyzer (Paris, Desclée & Brouwer, 1951–73).

Porphyry, *Porphyrii Isagoge et in Aristotelis Categorias Commentarium*, ed. by A. Busse, *Commentaria in Aristotelem Graeca 4, 1* (Berlin, G. Reimer, 1887).

Proclus, *Tria Opuscula*, ed. by H. Boese (Berlin, W. de Gruyter, 1960).

Rosenthal, F., 'Fīthāghūras', EI2, vol. 2, pp. 929–30.

Rosenthal, F., 'Some Pythagorean Documents transmitted in Arabic', *Orientalia* 10 (1941), pp. 104–15.

Ross, David, *Aristotle* (London, Methuen, 1964).

Rypka, J., *History of Iranian Literature* (Dordrecht, Reidel, 1968).

Schacht, J., 'Aḥmad', EI2, vol. 1, p. 267.

Schwarzbaum, H., 'Jewish, Christian, Moslem and Falasha Legends of the Death of Aaron, the High Priest', *Fabula* 5 (1962–63), pp. 185–227.

Scott, Walter, *Hermetica*, 4 vols (London, Dawsons of Pall Mall, 1968).

Seale, M. S., *Qur'an and Bible* (London, Croom Helm, 1978).

Shaban, M. A., *Islamic History: A.D. 600–750 (A.H. 132): a New Interpretation* (Cambridge, Cambridge University Press, 1971).

Shaban, M. A., *Islamic History: a New Interpretation 2: A.D. 750–1055 (A.H. 132–448)*, (Cambridge, Cambridge University Press, 1976).

Shorter Encyclopaedia of Islam, Ed. by H. A. R. Gibb and J. H. Kramers (Leiden, E. J. Brill/London, Luzac & Co., 1961).

Staniland, Hilary, *Universals* (New York, Doubleday, 1972).

Stern, S. M., 'Additional Notes to the Article: "The Authorship of the Epistles of the Ikhwān aṣ-Ṣafā" ', *Islamic Culture* 21 (1947), pp. 403–4.

Stern, S. M., 'The Authorship of the Epistles of the Ikhwān-aṣ-Ṣafā', *Islamic Culture* 20 (1946), pp. 367–72.

Stern, S. M., 'New Information about the Authors of the "Epistles of the Sincere Brethren" ', *Islamic Studies*, vol. 3, no. 4 (1964), pp. 405–28.

Stobaeus, John, *Ioannis Stobaei Anthologium*, vol. 1, ed. by C. Wachsmuth and Otto Hense (Berlin, Weidmann, 1958).

Subhan, John A., *Sufism: its Saints and Shrines* (New York, Samuel Weiser, 1970).

Sweetman, J. W., *Islam and Christian Theology*, pt 1, vol. 1, (London, Lutterworth Press, 1945).

Talmud, *Hebrew–English Edition of the Babylonian Talmud: Pesaḥim*, trans. by H. Freedman and ed. by I. Epstein (London, Soncino Press, 1967).

Taylor, A. E., *Aristotle*, (New York, Dover Publications/London, Constable, 1955).

Tibawi, A. L., 'The Idea of Guidance in Islam from an Educational Point of View', *Islamic Quarterly* vol. 3, no. 2 (1956), pp. 139–56.

Tibawi, A. L., 'Ikhwān aṣ-Ṣafā and their Rasā'il: a Critical Review of a Century and a Half of Research', *Islamic Quarterly*, vol. 2, no. 1 (1955), pp. 28–46.

Tibawi, A. L., 'Some Educational Terms in *Rasā'il Ikhwān aṣ-Ṣafā*', *Islamic Quarterly*, vol. 5, nos 1–2 (1959), pp. 55–60.

Ullmann, Manfred, *Islamic Medicine, Islamic Surveys 11* (Edinburgh, Edinburgh University Press, 1978).

Vajda, G., ''Azāzīl', EI2, vol. 1, p. 811.

Vajda, G., 'Idrīs', EI2, vol. 3, pp. 1030–1.
Von Grunebaum, G. E., *Medieval Islam* (Chicago and London, University of Chicago Press, 1966).
Wallis, R. T., *Neoplatonism* (London, Duckworth, 1972).
Walzer, R., 'Furfūriyūs', EI2, vol. 2, pp. 948–9.
Watt, W. Montgomery, 'The Camel and the Needle's Eye' in *Ex Orbe Religionum: Studia Geo Widengren Oblata*, vol. 2, ed. by C. J. Bleeker *et al.*, *Studies in the History of Religions XXII* (Leiden, E. J. Brill, 1972), pp. 155–8.
Watt, W. Montgomery, *Companion to the Qur'ān* (London, Allen & Unwin, 1967).
Watt, W. Montgomery, *Islamic Philosophy and Theology, Islamic Surveys 1* (Edinburgh, Edinburgh University Press, 1967).
Wensinck, A. J., 'al-Khaḍir (al-Khiḍr)', EI2, vol. 4, pp. 902–5.
Widengren, Geo, 'The Gnostic Technical Language in the Rasā'il Iḫwān al-Ṣafā'' in *Actas Do IV Congresso De Estudos Arabes E Islâmicos: Coimbra-Lisboa 1968* (Leiden, E. J. Brill, 1971), pp. 181–203.
Wilson, R. McL. (trans.), *The Gospel of Philip*, trans. from the Coptic text (London, A. R. Mowbray & Co., 1962).
Zaehner, R. C., *The Dawn and Twilight of Zoroastrianism* (London, Weidenfeld & Nicolson, 1961).

Index

In this Index the prefix '*al-*' has been omitted from proper names at the *beginning* of an entry.